Lust Busters

By Evan Keliher

Pedagogue Press P.O. Box 28808 San Diego, CA 92198

All rights reserved, no part of this book may be reproduced or transmitted in any form or by any means, electronic or mechanical, including photocopying, recording, or by any information storage and retrieval system without written permission from the author, except for the inclusion of brief quotations in a review.

ISBN # 978-0-9648859-9-8
SAN # 298-8054
Evan Keliher ©1989
Rev. Ed. 2010
Library of Congress Catalog
Card Number: 2009930521
Cover Design by Steve Lopez, Hemet, CA

Printed in the United States of America

Other works by Evan Keliher

Books

BOOMERS!
(A Survival Guide for the Future)

Grandpa's Marijuana Handbook

Guerrilla Warfare for Teachers

The De-Balling of America

Grandpa Ganja's
High School Survival Guide

Tyrannicide
The Story of the Second American Revolution

Videos/Films

Rebel High *(feature film)*
Montreal, Canada

My Lovely Bank *(sitcom pilot)*
Montreal, Canada

Grandpa's Marijuana Handbook *(the movie)*
San Diego, CA

Stage Plays

Sandwiched Light
Witte's End

See additional plays/screenplays/sitcoms
www.grandpaspotbook.com

CHAPTER ONE

The Beginning

It was pitch dark in a war zone. Parked cars loomed into view as darker smudges against the inky blackness of the night. I was huddled in a lump of humanity along with eight other guys all of whom were wearing bulky vests and helmets and carrying shotguns and licking dry lips in anticipation of some trauma or other waiting in the dark for them.

"Scared, Grogan?" a grizzled sergeant said.

"Why should I be scared?" I said, as I squirmed to stop my camera from gouging my ribs. "We're knocking over a dope den full of guys with Uzis. What could possibly happen?"

"'Atta boy. Stay close. I'll make you look like Ansel Adams."

All of a sudden the doors popped open and everybody leapt from the van and raced toward a decrepit Victorian house with a long porch across its front and a lot of shrubbery around it. Whistles sounded and shouts of "Police!" rang out as they stormed the place.

I followed close on the heels of the sergeant in a mad, confused run in the dark when I heard loud popping sounds as the dope dealers opened fire on the cops and the cops returned fire. I looked toward the house and when I looked back the sergeant was gone and I was alone.

Bullets were flying everywhere. Some ricocheted off the sidewalk and sailed off in crazy directions and I knew precipitous action was called for so I dove around the corner of the porch and rolled to my feet in a single, fluid motion and looked wildly around for sanctuary. There wasn't any sanctuary but there was a huge guy wearing a backwards baseball cap and a scowl that would intimidate Hulk Hogan. He also had a sawed-off shotgun.

Calling on all my years' experience as a quick-thinking big city news reporter, I thought fast and shouted, "Hold it!" I raised my camera, fired off a shot and the flash blinded the guy and gave me time to duck and run the other way. I took about four steps when something hit me in the back and knocked me ass over apple cart into the shrubbery. I grimaced in pain and struggled out of my bulletproof vest and held it up to examine the three rips where the slugs struck it.

"Holy shit!" I said. Then, "I gotta get some pictures!"

I held the camera up above porch level and fired off a series of quick shots in half-a-dozen directions and was greeted by a hail of bullets from the dope dealers in reply. I lowered the camera and looked for a way out.

"Strike two!" I said. "That does it. I quit!"

I ran like a steeplechase runner for about three blocks and leapt over trashcans and debris as I went. I hailed a cab and made it back to the station where I retrieved my car and went home to reflect on things.

The next day I sent my stuff in to the paper and

had a leisurely breakfast and enjoyed a cigar on a park bench in the next block. I headed for the Trib about ten-thirty and once arrived I marched across the city room and entered the glass-enclosed office with the word EDITOR on the door.

"Good work, Grogan," Pete said. "You've got some great pictures here and a bang-up story. We're givin' it a three column spread and..."

"I quit."

"You what?"

"I said I quit."

"Some other time, eh, Grogan? I got a paper to run here."

"I mean it. I'm going to write a book."

"You're quittin' to write a book? Are you nuts?"

"Yeah, like that wily fox. I could've been killed last night, Pete. Think about it. That's a helluva concept, isn't it? Well, I don't need it. I'm heading for some nice, quiet little town where nothing ever happens and I'm going to write a real book and win the Pulitzer Prize. So I quit."

I started for the door and Pete shouted, "You are nuts! You'll starve out there! You'll be crawlin' back here before the week is out!"

As I rode the elevator down and out of the Trib Building for the very last time, I spoke out in a voice so loud I startled myself. "Fuck you, Pete," I said, "I'm gonna get myself a Pulitzer Prize."

CHAPTER TWO

A Nice, Quiet, Little Town

Midvale wasn't much of a town but it was just what I was looking for. If a man couldn't concentrate on his work in a place as dull and ordinary as this burg, why, he'd have to be afflicted with some sort of attention-deficit disorder — or so I remember thinking at the time. Little did I know that Midvale would enjoy worldwide infamy in the next few months and change my own and thousands (millions?) of other lives forever.

I stood on the sidewalk in front of the Midvale Beacon and studied its facade in the warm April sun while inhaling the delicate aroma of ink and newsprint that filled the air for yards in every direction. It was a familiar smell, one I'd breathed for fifteen years in widely scattered ports of call, and it was made all the more familiar by equal parts of cigar smoke, stale beer, and half-eaten bologna sandwiches. It was a smell found nowhere else in Christendom and one I truly loved.

I went in and found a long counter separating the work area from the common rabble that might wander in with business to conduct. A few scattered wooden chairs, a table, and a very old cat made up the furniture of the lobby. A hallway led off toward the rear of the place and a stairway behind the counter rose to the second floor. There was a hum of machinery that

I could feel more than actually hear and I knew the presses were rolling.

A woman in the neighborhood of sixty or so was crouched behind the counter and she looked up when I entered. "Yes?" she said. She made it sound more like an interrogation than an offer to help.

"Name's Grogan," I said, "Jack Grogan. I have an appointment with Mr. Zeckerdorf." She seemed dubious so I added, "For nine-thirty."

"You're the new reporter."

"Yes."

"Mr. Zeckerdorf isn't in. Here. He said you should go cover Ed Beckett's auction. It's out on Mill Road."

She tossed a scrap of yellow legal pad on the counter and returned to her work. I picked up the paper and saw the name Ed Beckett and an address on it.

"Uh, can you tell me exactly where Ed's place is?" I said.

"Just ask anybody," she said without looking up.

"I thought I was," I said. She looked up and I shrugged and started for the door.

Outside on the sidewalk, I saw a freckle-faced kid coming along and I asked him for directions to Ed's place.

"Second right and then left," he said. "Go eight miles out Plank Road and right on Mill. It's half-a-mile down Mill."

Twenty minutes later I turned on Mill as instructed and drove past acres of green stuff about ten inches high. I didn't recognize it but knew it wasn't an orchard, as I knew fruit trees were usually a bit taller than ten inches. The green stuff ran smack up against an enormous barn and about twenty pickups that were parked nearby. There were more trucks parked along the road itself and I pulled in behind them, climbed out, and joined the men assembled in the barnyard.

These guys all wore striped overalls, the kind with the bibs. Flannel shirts, heavy work shoes, and baseball caps with words like John Deere and Pennzoil on them completed their ensembles and informed the uninitiated that he was dealing with genuine farmers. They stood about in knots and spat tobacco juice this way and that and looked knowingly out at the fields of green stuff and stole covetous glances at the pile of rusted metal that was to be auctioned.

Never having seen actual farmers so close up before, I was duly impressed. Here was the real article, husbandmen of the soil, the guys who put my bran flakes on the table every morning, the last bastion of real America against the relentless inroads of technology and modernism. It was a stirring moment for me, one that I wouldn't soon forget.

But I was here as a reporter and reporting was what I'd do, so I decided to eavesdrop on some of them to get the drift of their opinions and measure the cut of their jibs, so to speak. I sidled up to one group standing in large patches of what even I recognized as manure and looked out knowingly at the green stuff. I overheard the following conversation.

"He says it was Edie Hawkins, all right."

"Edie? You sure, Duke?"

"Damn right I'm sure," Duke said. "Jake says Pete saw them with his own eyes."

"Who woulda thought Edie Hawkins'd get mixed

up with a guy like Sims?"

Another guy shook his head and said, "You never know. Women do a lot of crazy things. 'Member Sarah Waters and that dentist over in Elkind? Now there was a strange pair."

"Shit, she only went with him 'cause he was makin' her bridge for free."

"'Member the school teacher an' Dick Beckman's hired hand?" another wit chimed in. "She was engaged to marry that lawyer over in Tonopah an' she was layin' the hired hand in Dick's barn right up to the day of the weddin.'"

Duke shook his head. "Oh, she was no good, all right."

"Well, the guy was a lawyer, wasn't he?" another said. "Serves the bastard right, I say. How many innocent people has he screwed?"

The others muttered and murmured agreement and spat tobacco juice and gazed out on the green stuff and I moseyed off in search of some signs of intelligent life.

A few minutes later the auctioneer pulled up in his own pickup and clambered out. He sauntered out among the rusted machinery scattered around the farmyard and made an on-the-spot analysis of its probable worth and asking price. A gaggle of farmers trailed along behind feigning indifference in these same items even as they mentally calculated how little they could steal them for.

The whole thing was depressing as hell; at least it was at first. I mean, watching some poor bastard lose his farm and sell off his equipment had become a modern American tragedy and I remarked as much to a local standing next to me.

"Ed ain't losin' no farm," he said indignantly. "Shit, Ed's got more'n a thousand acres right here an' he owns another farm just like this'n over in Gogebic County." He pointed off to his left. "That's his car over there by the chicken coop."

I looked in the direction indicated and saw the front end of a sleek black Mercedes glistening in the morning sunlight. So much for my depression over the plight of the poor American farmer.

Anyway, Ed and the auctioneer took up their places and the sale was underway. The auctioneer filled the air with nonsense syllables and the farmers spat and coveted and piece-by-piece the pile of rusted machinery was sold for astonishing prices. I mean, the stuff must have had some intrinsic value that was quite hidden to the layman but was obvious to a farmer or they'd never have paid such prices, but I swear I know rust when I see it and they sure as hell were buying rust.

For instance, there was a big iron gadget with a lot of little steel wheels on it that looked like the round blades of a butcher's saw and the damned thing went for almost three grand. I looked to see if the guy who bought it had a look in his eye that might indicate he was the town half-wit but he seemed at least as smart as the rest of them. As I said, the value was probably intrinsic.

After the last item was sold, a lot of bottles were produced from various back pockets and the farmers proceeded to get half smashed while a lot of farm animals cackled, mooed, grunted, and belched and the green stuff steadily advanced on the farmhouse from all sides. One of them offered me a swig but the thought of a whiskey bottle passed among a lot of guys still chewing tobacco was aesthetically unappetizing so I declined on the grounds that it was only nine-thirty and I hadn't had breakfast yet.

"Nine-thirty an' you ain't had breakfast yet?" the old coot said incredulously. He laughed and others nearby joined him in sharing a good time at my expense. I learned later that these guys routinely ate breakfast at five a.m. sharp and thought everybody else did, too. Isn't that amazing?

I stopped and chatted with Ed Beckett for a minute and made a few suggestions as to how he might improve the overall quality of life on his farm and I must say he was so grateful he was actually speechless. I assured him it was nothing and thanked him for not becoming effusive in his appreciation and headed back to town.

Back at the Beacon I learned Mr. Zeckerdorf hadn't returned yet so I commandeered an idle computer and wrote up my story on Ed Beckett's auction.

It was a real zinger of a story, too, with lots of pep and color I knew would appeal to the townsfolk. I finished it just in time for inclusion in the Thursday edition as they were locking in the presses when I handed it in.

I went out for an early lunch (or a late breakfast) and strolled down Main Street to Lola's cafe, a local eatery with lots of rural atmosphere including red and white checkered plastic tablecloths and a long lunch counter with stools that always seemed to be occupied by the same guys. Cigarette smoke filled the air and a country n' western tune of indistinguishable origin emanated from a jukebox in a corner. Apparently the anti-smoking trend had missed Midvale entirely.

I sat down at a table and Lola herself approached with a coffee pot and a menu. She poured coffee and said, "You're the new reporter Bert hired over at the Beacon, right?"

"Right," I said. "How'd you know that?"

"News travels fast around here. By the time the Beacon gets it, it isn't news any longer."

"I guess you heard about Ed Beckett's auction then?" I said.

"You mean about Edie Hawkins and that Sims fella?" she said. "Sure. Whole town knows about them."

"Do Edie and Sims know the whole town knows?" I asked.

"Well, everybody except Pete Hawkins and Janie Sims. 'Course, nobody tells them about it. We aren't troublemakers, you know."

Feeling somewhat redundant, I ordered Lola's special fat-free breakfast that consisted of a four-egg omelet, four links of sausage, biscuits and gravy, and a side order of hashed browns washed down with a tankard of hot coffee. Thus fortified, I wandered off along Main Street to look the town over and get my bearings.

Midvale had its pool hall, several gas stations, a firehouse, two supermarkets, a City Hall, a department store, three or four strip malls with drugstores, cleaners, and whatnot interspersed here and there, and a population of about ten thousand souls who used the services provided by the aforementioned. It was largely clean and tidy and without crime or violence, on the whole an altogether pleasant little burg situated nearly eighty miles from the nearest mid-sized city.

It was also an old town with a shaky economy based on cows, fields of green stuff, and Saturday night truck rodeos. Young people instinctively lit out for the big city as soon as they could and the population declined steadily as a result.

It was, in fact, an unlikely place for a world traveler like me. I'd practiced the trade of journalism in cities as large as Chicago and L.A. and even did a stint as a foreign correspondent in Central America. I was an old pro who'd experienced the best and worst of the profession, but I hadn't satisfied a longstanding ambition to write the Great American Novel, a sickness that afflicts every wordsmith to a greater or lesser degree, and I resolved to retire to some bucolic setting far from the sturm und drang of big city cares and write the book that would earn me a Pulitzer Prize and enormous sums of money in one fell swoop.

So here I was in Midvale, a reporter on a twice-weekly sheet that served a cross section of small town America. Surely, I'd be able to do some serious writing in a place as serene and calm as Midvale—or so I thought.

I chanced across a real estate office on the corner of Elm and Main and stepped inside to see if they had something I might rent. A woman about thirty or so was working at a desk and I saw at once that she was pretty, nicely dressed, and that her short skirt was riding high enough on her shapely thigh to attract the notice of all but the totally blind. She looked up and saw me watching her thighs and she vainly tugged her skirt downward.

"May I help you?" she said.

"You already have," I said, smiling.

"Oh. You're the new man at the Beacon."

I shook my head and sighed. "Yeah, but it's plain they didn't need me. People around here get the news before it even happens."

She smiled and said, "I guess we do at that. And I also guess you need a place to stay."

"Right again. Something cheap. Journalism is one of the least rewarding professions, you know."

"Furnished or unfurnished?"

"Furnished. I never stay long enough to acquire furniture."

"No wife? Family?"

"Nope. Just me and my computer."

"I think I have just the thing," she said, opening a file cabinet and rummaging through it. "It's right here in town, it's clean and it's furnished. Three rooms. It's above the town pool hall."

"There must be a catch," I said. "Apartments over pool halls don't come cheap."

"I thought the pool hall might make it undesirable," she said.

"Are you kidding? I thought I'd have to pay extra. I love pool halls. You meet great people in pool halls."

"Good. The rent's only three hundred a month. First and last in advance. Would you like to see it?"

"No, I'll take it. If it's got a pool hall, how can I go wrong?"

She stood up and her skirt dropped until it was only about four inches above her knee and broad expanses of flashing nylon-clad thigh showed as she moved. She crossed to a cabinet and got a set of keys.

"You can make the check out to Krogh's real estate. I'm Ellen Krogh."

She extended her hand and I took it. "Jack Grogan," I said. "The pleasure's mine."

And so I acquired not only a place to stay during my sojourn in Midvale, but also the acquaintance of a refreshingly attractive young lady who was probably married to some bruiser who's hobby was maiming guys who looked askance at his wife.

Ah, well. I stopped by the apartment and examined my new digs. The lady was as good as her word. The place was clean, it had a living room, kitchen, and bedroom, and it did have a pool hall under it.

I went in the pool hall on my way out and felt I'd stepped back twenty-five years through a time warp of some kind to my sadly misspent youth. I half expected to hear the Twilight Zone theme song and Rod Serling setting the scene for another episode.

There were six tables and they were actually covered with green felt instead of pastel blues and pinks. There were cuspidors against the walls and old-fashioned green-shaded light bulbs over the tables with the light falling in such a way that the rest of the room was clothed in near darkness. Figures stepping into and out of the light seemed to appear and disappear magically.

High stools standing along the walls and a beer cooler next to the glass counter made up the furniture.

An old guy wearing tattoos and a stiff straw boater sat hunched over the counter smoking a cigar and scanning a Racing Form.

The name Andy's was spelled out in backward neon letters on the window with Billiards below it. Two guys were playing eight ball on the first table. I approached the counter.

"You must be Andy," I said.

The old guy looked at me. "Nope. Andy's dead. I'm Nick."

"I'm sorry about Andy..." I started to say.

"It's okay. He died in '58. Folks around here stop grievin' after fifty years."

"Well," I said, buoyed by this news, "I'm glad Andy's been dead so long then. My name's..."

"Grogan. You're the new man over at the Beacon."

"Yeah, right. Anyway, I just rented the place upstairs so I guess we'll be neighbors."

"Try to keep the noise down, will ya?" Nick said. "We run a quiet place here an' people'll get pissed-off if you go jumpin' around up there an' carryin' on."

"What?" I said. "Disturb a pool hall? Never. You can trust me. I'm a gentleman of the old school when it comes to proper behavior in and around pool halls. Why, I regard a well-run pool hall as I do a well-run cathedral, a place due man's respect, even awe. The pool hall is the only place you can find the few remaining individualists left out there and I'd be the last to disturb one of them."

Nick eyed me narrowly for a moment, then grinned and stuck out his hand. "If you write like you talk, you're gonna be okay, Grogan."

"Good, because I write exactly as I talk," I said. "And speaking of writing, I'd better get back to the Beacon. I still haven't met the boss yet."

"Here, have a cigar," Nick said as I started out.

"Is it like the one you're smoking?" I asked.

"Yep."

"Then no thanks. I prefer my cigars made with real tobacco."

I headed back to the Beacon and congratulated myself on a very successful first day. I'd already covered my first story, rented an apartment, met a pretty woman, and befriended the proprietor of the town's leading pool hall. Not bad at all.

Mr. Zeckerdorf still hadn't returned when I got there about one o'clock so I decided to hang around and meet some of my fellow employees. A few minutes later a young kid about nineteen came in and stopped short when he saw me.

"Oh," he said. Then, "Are you Mr. Grogan?"

"You mean you don't know?" I said. "If not, you're the only guy in town who doesn't know my pedigree in its entirety."

"I'm Amos Cooper," he said. "Copyboy. I'm a journalism major at State."

"Great career choice, Amos—if you're inured to poverty. Who else you got on staff?"

"Well, there's Tom and Al, they work in the print shop. And Marti, she's part-time, goes to Midvale High. Ada Hasp runs the office and our other reporter is Art Fazer, he's over in Tonopah covering Dick Oster's funeral."

"And Dick Oster was...?"

"He owned the McDonald's over there."

"I see." I looked at my watch. "When's the paper come out?"

"Any minute now. Come on, you can meet Tom and Al and we'll see if the paper's ready."

He headed for the back and I followed him.

Tom and Al wore baseball caps, T-shirts, and about a gallon of ink each. "Hey, you guys, this is Jack Grogan," Amos said. "He's the new reporter. Jack, this is Tom and Al."

"My pleasure, boys," I said, shaking hands and then looking for a rag to wipe off the ink.

"Got your piece in today's paper," Tom said. He handed me a copy of the Beacon opened to the second page and there it was just as I'd written it. "Good job."

"Thanks," I said, "but it isn't so much, really. Just a routine story, nothing special."

"Bert hasn't seen it yet, has he?" Al asked.

"Bert?"

"Mr. Zeckerdorf," Amos said. "Everybody calls him Bert."

"I guess not. He wasn't in when I got here."

"He'll probably mention it when he gets in," Tom said, and he grinned at Al who grinned back.

I found out what was so funny an hour later when Bert finally showed up and invited me into his office for a chat. He was about seventy and he wore a cheap suit with red suspenders over a dress shirt with a clip-on bow tie. I had a feeling he'd worn the suspenders a lot of years before they became fashionable again since he looked like the kind of guy who'd welcome change about like a colony of Shakers.

"Saw your story," he said. "Nice piece of writin,' too."

"Thanks," I said. "First time out I wasn't sure I'd get everything just right, but I guess I did."

"Oh, you did fine, just fine. 'Course, there are a couple of things to look out for next time." He picked up the paper from his desk and looked at it. "For example, that 'green stuff' you mention bein' all around Ed's farm. That's alfalfa, you know."

"It is? I mean, it is. Sure. And as nice a crop as I've ever seen, too."

"And another thing. Ed wasn't sellin' antiques; it was farm machinery."

"What? Why, I'd have sworn it was a lot of modern art. Most of that stuff looked like Picasso designed it on a bad day. I've seen sculptures just like those in every farmer's fields for miles around."

Bert shook his head. "They're not sculptures, just farm machinery. Farmers leave 'em in the fields until they need 'em again and they get a little rusty."

The old guy reached into a desk drawer and came up with a bottle of bourbon and a couple of glasses and proceeded to fill them up. He handed me one and picked up the other one. "To alfalfa and modern art," he said.

"Salud," I said, and tossed it down.

"I like it, Grogan," he said. "Keep it up."

"Keep what up?"

"The naive city slicker stuff. You know, pretendin' to be ignorant about country things like callin' alfalfa 'green stuff' and mistakin' farm machinery for modern art. It'll get people buyin' papers just to see what dumb thing you might say next."

"Oh, that," I said. "I'm a pro, Mr. Zeckerdorf. I'm always thinking of ways to increase circulation. After all, isn't that what journalism's all about?"

"Call me Bert," he said, grinning. "I like your style, Grogan."

"And I yours, Bert," I said.

And so it was that I settled into the daily routine of Midvale for what I thought was going to be an idyllic period of my life during which I'd write that big novel—or a reasonable facsimile thereof. As I said, it was going to be something more than that before this saga ended and I didn't have to wait long for things to heat up.

CHAPTER THREE

The Rolls-Royce Woman

In the next few weeks I met all of the town's dignitaries and came to be regarded almost as a regular at the places where the power brokers of Midvale held forth such as the firehouse, City Hall, Lola's, and a bar called Brady's that had moose heads and stuffed fish on the walls with pre-Spanish-American war dust all over them. I numbered the chief of police, the mayor, all six councilmen, the city attorney, assorted cops and local businessmen and various hangers-on among my personal acquaintances.

I even gained a certain notoriety with my writing. After each edition of the Beacon, farmers would gather in groups and have a laugh at the expense of "that Grogan fella." Circulation actually did go up after my arrival, a fact that wasn't lost on Bert. He regularly encouraged me to continue the "ruse" and I took credit for it even though none of it was really feigned ignorance. I mean, what the hell was I supposed to know about esoteric things like alfalfa and the innerworkings of silos, hen houses, haymows, and animal husbandry?

Anyway, after I'd been in town about a month or so, I was supervising a checker game at the firehouse during one of the frequent lulls which befell Midvale when a white Rolls-Royce turned the corner and sailed past like some gliding ghost caught inadvertently in daylight and anxious to find sanctuary in a dark corner somewhere.

"Hey, that's a Rolls-Royce," I said.

Everybody looked up and watched the elegant car pass the firehouse and turn the corner.

"A Rolls-Royce?" Phil Botts said.

"What's a Rolls doin' in Midvale?" Zack Oates said.

"Passin' through, I reckon," Sy Mellers said. "Must be 'cause this town don't have no Rolls-Royces."

I stared absently after the car and uttered what later would be recalled as prophetic words. "I'll bet there's a story in a car like that."

"Yeah," Zack said, "an' I'll bet it's got somethin' to do with the Devil. Regular people don't drive Rolls-Royces."

"If it's the Devil he must be female then," I said. "That was a woman driving it."

"A woman?" Sy said. "What's a woman doin' in a car like that?"

"Humph," Phil said, "must be some rich guy's floozie. How else'd she get herself a Rolls-Royce, for Christ's sake?"

"Spoken like a true troglodyte, Phil," I said. "Did it ever occur to you she might have earned it?"

"Yeah, that's what I said," he replied. "She must be some rich guy's floozie."

Everybody laughed at that and went back to the checker game but I decided I'd had enough firehouse humor for the nonce and headed down Oak Street and around the corner to Main to see if I could learn what happened to the Rolls.

I found it at Bud's gas station where Bud himself was pumping gas into it and his two helpers were busily washing the car's windows and flicking imaginary dust from its already immaculate finish while shooing away a lot of kids who gaped in awe at the sight and hesitantly leaned in to touch a cautious finger to the car.

The windows were opaque on the sides and rear and it was impossible to see who was driving it from that vantage point so I ambled on past to the corner and looked back through the windshield. A woman wearing a wide-brimmed hat that nearly covered her face searched through her purse with head bent so I couldn't get a good look at her.

Bud replaced the hose and went to the driver's window. The woman paid him and started the car and drove off. Bud stood there with his outstretched hand holding the money and stared after her with a vacant look on his mug and his mouth hanging open like a sprung trap door.

The car went to the corner and pulled in to the curb in front of the Midvale Manor, the town's leading hotel that stood just across from the Beacon. A crowd of gawkers quickly formed up and gaped in reverential silence at the spectacle before them. Since it was only half a block away, I managed to reach the hotel when the car door opened and I found myself gazing into the sexiest pair of eyes ever beheld by man.

Her eyes locked briefly on mine and I felt my knees buckle and a flush suffuse my cheeks. I stood transfixed as her skirt rode high on her thigh when she swung a long, imperially slim leg out of the car and placed a delicately shod high heel on the pavement. A hushed murmur rose from the men and boys who stood around me and it was accompanied by a hissing sound as the women and girls involuntarily drew in their collective breath in a reaction one might expect if they'd seen Satan himself climb out.

There was a momentary pause before the other leg joined its mate and the view provided in the interim was enough to inflame a eunuch on pension. A moment more and she emerged from the car and stood up while her skirt slid back down in place and an even louder murmur swept the crowd and the hissing intensified at the sight of her.

She was strikingly, astonishingly beautiful. Everything was perfect. Cheek bones. Nose. Full mouth. Hair. All perfect. Her eyes seemed an affront, challenging and daring and sardonic at once. Eyes that snapped and sparkled and laughed out loud.

She was beautiful, all right, but more than that she was sexy. I mean, the woman looked like she bathed in liquid hormones and she filled the air with sultry gusts of pheromones that shot into every male brain like a jolt of electricity and caused eyes to bulge and nostrils to flare. She was tall and slim, elegantly dressed and coifed, and possessed of incredible breasts that pressed perky nipples against a thin silk blouse, but there was something more, much more, about her that stirred atavistic desires in every man who laid eyes on her.

The woman was sex personified, a walking monument to things carnal and forbidden—and irresistible.

Every man there, including small boys not yet men who knew instinctively they were beholding something remarkable, gazed rapturously at her and followed her every move with unwavering attention.

Even the women were struck by her beauty and blinding sexuality but for very different reasons and with different reactions. To them, she was evil incarnate, dangerous and threatening and sinister, and they watched her with fear and loathing and continued the low hissing sounds like a lot of cats warily eyeing a newcomer to the neighborhood.

A moment later the Rolls-Royce woman, as she came to be called, disappeared into the hotel and left us gawking on the sidewalk after her like a lot of schoolboys mesmerized in front of the fan dancer's tent at a carnival. The women came to their senses first and rudely jerked the rest of us back to reality.

"Well, I never!" one woman said.

"Me, neither, but I'll bet she has!" another remarked.

One woman grabbed her husband by the arm and gave him a good shake.

"What the hell are you lookin' at?" she demanded. "Go on, get along there!" She gave the hapless guy a shot that propelled him headlong down the sidewalk and nearly into Chief Hawes who'd just arrived on the scene.

Hawes saw the assembled gawkers and said, "What's goin' on, Grogan?"

"I don't know for sure, Chief," I said, "but either I've just seen the sexiest creature in the whole world or I've gone over the edge at last."

"You ain't batty," a farmer said. "Look."

He pointed at the other guys in the vicinity and every man present looked like he had a gun in his pocket and a quick glance assured me I was similarly armed. One old guy in his eighties studied his nether parts with a happy grin plastered on his face and sang out, "It's up! The dang thing's up! Hey, Martha! I got it up again!"

"Shit, this I gotta see," the Chief said, and he started into the hotel to look for himself.

I saw Ellen Krogh coming toward me and I turned away and reached into my pocket to reorient things before I had to face her and expose my delicate condition. I mean, how does one tactfully explain a full-blown hard-on at high noon on a public thoroughfare?

"Hi, Jack," she said. "Who owns the Rolls?"

I looked at the car and said absently, "Aphrodite."

"Who?"

"Oh. I mean, I don't know. Just some woman. I think she's new in town."

"She must be. That's got to be the only Rolls in Midvale."

"Anyway, how's the real estate business?"

"Slow, but it always is here. Had lunch yet? I was just going to Lola's for a sandwich. I hate to eat alone and I seem to do a lot of that lately."

"Well, you'll not eat alone today, fair lady. Let's go."

We started for Lola's and I kept one hand in my pocket to make sure things didn't get out of hand, as it were. We were just crossing the street when I looked back and saw Chief Hawes emerging from the hotel with his hat held strategically in front of him. He caught my eye and blinked in disbelief.

We ran into Eli Grimes in Lola's. Eli was about fifty or so; he owned the town lumber yard and served as Midvale's mayor. Eli had the crafty look of the politician, the same shifty eyes and phony smile and oily, ingratiating manner which stamp all politicians and he was no intellectual powerhouse, but he was likable enough and probably no more crooked than the average man in the street—which is to say he should be serving time somewhere.

"I liked your story on the council meetin,' Grogan," he said. "It was fair and accurate."

"I just report the facts, Mr. Mayor," I said.

"Eli," he said with a broad smile, "call me Eli. We don't stand on ceremony in Midvale; we're all just one big happy family around here. Isn't that right, Ellen? We've got the best little town in the whole country right here in Midvale, a town where every man knows his neighbor and everybody knows him and we're damn proud of it."

"And well you should be," I said. "People in big cities like L.A. or New York don't know what they're missing. Why, they think art museums and theatres and trendy bars and major league ballgames and anonymity can provide as good a lifestyle as having lunch at Lola's, hanging around the firehouse, and everybody in town knowing everybody else on sight."

"Damn right," Eli said. "Listen, you stop by my office and we'll have lunch, you hear? I always like to keep a good workin' relationship with the press, know what I mean?"

"I always say we need each other, Eli," I grinned at him. "Know what I mean?"

He grinned back. "I sure do. Don't forget now."

He moved on to some old codgers ensconced on stools at the counter and was soon laughing heartily at some rustic witticism. Ellen smiled her own smile then.

"I've noticed you're rather fond of wry humor," she said.

"Who, me? Wry? Whatever do you mean?"

"You know what I mean. Comparing this town to L.A. You ought to be ashamed of yourself."

"I'm only half wry. Don't forget, L.A. also has rampant drug use and drive-by shootings and smog and a lot of other things people can do without."

"We may not have all that but people die of boredom every day around here. Sometimes I'm not sure dying in a drive-by shooting is any worse than dying of boredom."

"Good point. It is slow around here, isn't it?"

"Too slow. We need some excitement, anything. The biggest event all last year was when Jake McAllister's barn burned down and Barney Hoke drove the fire truck into Paint Creek. The Beacon ran stories on that for three weeks straight."

"But that's why I came here in the first place," I said. "I've got the time to work on my novel now. No distractions."

"You're writing a novel? How's it coming along?"

"Great. I'm all the way up to chapter one. At this rate I'll have it finished in a decade or two if I'm lucky."

Lola showed up then and said, "Hear that Rolls-

Royce woman raised quite a fuss over at the hotel. Ed Bower said she vamped every man who saw her."

"Well, I saw her and she didn't vamp me," I said defensively.

Lola shrugged. "Ed said the Chief saw her and when he came out he tripped and almost pole-vaulted over the flower boxes they got there."

"What's this?" Ellen said, smiling. "A mystery woman in a Rolls? Maybe this is just what we needed to add a little excitement to our town."

"She's probably just passing through," I said. "Be on her way out of town tomorrow."

"What'll it be?" Lola asked.

"Two tuna sandwiches on toast and coffee," I said.

"Make mine no caffeine," Ellen said.

Lola left and Ellen looked at me. "Was she really that sexy?" she said.

I sighed and said, "All I can say is, I'm glad I didn't trip. I'd have set an outdoor record with room to spare."

"I think I'd like to meet her."

"No, you wouldn't. Take my word for it."

She smiled and didn't say anything and Lola brought our coffee.

So I found out Ellen didn't have a bruiser of a husband and a light began to flicker in my eyes, the same one I thought I saw flickering in hers. Well. Maybe Midvale wouldn't be as dull as I thought.

CHAPTER FOUR

The Mystery Deepens

The Rolls-Royce woman didn't leave town after all. In fact, she settled in at the hotel in the largest suite they had, three rooms on the sixth-floor with a panoramic view of downtown Midvale, and gave every indication that she'd be around for a while. This news brought delight to the town's males and despair to the females, of course.

Fortunately, she stayed in her suite most of the time and it was a good thing she did because every time she ventured out she threw the whole town into an uproar. Men turned to gape at her and walked into mailboxes and barber poles and each other as though hypnotized.

They reacted this way every time, too. I mean, if a guy saw her leaving the hotel he'd stare slack-jawed and bug-eyed until she passed from view, and if he saw her again an hour later coming out of Kaz's drugstore he was entranced all over again and rendered a complete sap once more.

Two days after she arrived I was standing on the sidewalk talking to Chief Hawes and city attorney Carl Parks when she rounded the corner and approached us. The Chief saw her first and his lower jaw dropped and the by now familiar glazed look showed in his eye and I knew she was in the vicinity.

Carl and I both turned to look and the three of us stood there like a trio of punch drunk pugs trying to get a grip on the real world.

As she drew abreast of us she seemed to hesitate ever so slightly, then she looked at us and smiled a smile that dripped lust and desire and passion and all three of us leaned forward ready and willing to do her bidding whatever it might be. Then she moved on and crossed the street and disappeared around the next corner and she left the usual wake of stunned males staring after her with enormous pistols in their pockets.

Chief Hawes looked down and said, "Sonofabitch. She did it again."

"There's something funny about that lady," Carl said.

"Then why aren't you laughing?" I said.

"I don't mean funny funny, I mean strange funny. No woman should be that sexy."

"Or maybe they all should," I said.

"Are you kiddin'?" the Chief said. "Nobody'd work anymore. We'd spend all our time gettin' laid."

"Yeah," Carl said absently. He looked longingly in the direction of the disappeared Rolls-Royce woman and chewed his lip thoughtfully.

"Yeah," I said.

"Yeah," the Chief said.

We stared en masse and ruminated on the possibilities of a world where all women were wild, wanton creatures driven by libidos the size of our own and might be there still if the Rev. Skaggs hadn't come by then.

"So, gentlemen," he said, his very tone jolting us from our reveries, "I see that harlot's passed this way recently." He looked down meaningfully at the evidence standing tall for all to see.

"I can't deny it, Mr. Skaggs," I said. "We were standing here minding our own business when she came along and blinded us with a cloud of pheromones strong enough to turn on the lights."

"She's an evil woman," Skaggs said sternly. "There's lust in her eyes and heart, and she brings out lustful thoughts in others."

"Surely not preachers, too, Mr. Skaggs," I said, aghast.

He blushed and said, "That's how I know she's evil. We religiosos are trained to resist temptation but no one can resist that woman. I say she's been sent from Hell to tempt Midvale, and I say this town won't be safe until she's driven out."

"We can't do that, Mr. Skaggs," Carl said. "She's not breaking any laws. It isn't her fault if she turns people on, that's their problem."

"But there are laws and there are laws, Mr. Parks. She's breaking God's law because she's in league with Satan whom God hath cast out of Heaven and consigned to the nether world. Anyone who works with Satan is automatically God's enemy and a breaker of His laws."

"Maybe so, but you can't take that into court," Carl said. "She has her rights, too, you know."

"We'll see about that," Skaggs said icily. He drew himself up haughtily and strode off down the sidewalk.

"Now she's in for it, by God," the Chief said. "Skaggs'll have every old bat in the county on her ass before the week's out."

"If she keeps it up, she'll have every guy in the county on her ass before that," I said.

Carl got a faraway look in his eye again and said, "Yeah, and I hope I'm one of them."

"Me, too."

"Me, too."

Drawn by the same irresistible force, three very movable objects drifted off as one in the direction taken by the Rolls-Royce woman in hopes of having our own petards hoist once more.

By the end of the second day, she was the talk of the town. Most people still hadn't seen her in the flesh, but they'd heard eyewitness accounts from friends who knew someone who had seen her and that was enough to fire their imaginations. Crowds began forming outside the hotel in hopes of catching a glimpse of this wondrous creature and some confusion resulted. They followed her when she went abroad—though from a discreet distance since many people were vaguely afraid of her—and mini-traffic snarls occurred.

Some people demanded to know why the police weren't better able to control things but the answer should have been obvious. The cops no sooner got a glimpse of her than they turned into helpless masses of nerve endings totally unable to act in any other way than as frustrated would-be lovers stunned into inaction by their own libidos.

In fact, Bert wanted me to interview her and do a piece for the Beacon, but I was no more able to cope with her rampant sensuality than the cops.

"How can I interview her when my mind goes blank as soon as I see her?" I demanded. "One glimpse and my mind is filled with visions of pudenda and long, slim legs and creamy thighs and heaving boobs and nicely rounded buttocks and wild, orgiastic scenes full of heat and passion and low moaning sounds mixed with cries of pleasure and..."

I was carried away by the wonder of it all and unable to stop until Bert reached out and grabbed my lapels and gave me a good shake.

"Get a grip on yourself, Grogan!" he said.

I came to my senses and waved him off. "See? Just thinking about her turns me into a mindless wreck."

"Maybe Art could..."

"No, Art couldn't. And Amos can't. And you can't. Once she lets fly with those pheromones, we're all dick, period."

"I've got it!" Bert said. "We'll send Ada. She hasn't even got a dick."

"Might work," I said shrugging. "The only problem is, women don't like her much and I don't think she likes them, either."

"So what? I'm not askin' her to be her best friend, am I? All I want is an interview for Thursday's edition. Come on, let's go ask her."

So Ada agreed to do it. She grabbed a notebook and left straightaway for the hotel and Bert and I dropped by Brady's across the street to await results.

We'd hardly lit up a couple of cheroots and started in on a cold beer when Bert looked out the front window and saw Ada going back toward the Beacon.

"Hey!" he said. "It's Ada. She's goin' back to the Beacon."

"Jesus, that's either the fastest interview on record or she got thrown out. Come on, let's go see what happened."

We downed our beers and left. When we got to the office Ada was already at her desk pouring a double shot of her lumbago medicine into a water glass.

She looked pissed.

"Hey, what the hell happened?" Bert said. "Did you get the interview?"

"Hell, no, I didn't get the interview, and I'm not gonna, either," Ada said. "I wanted to break her skinny neck as soon as I laid eyes on her. Oh, she's a hard one, she is. A real ball buster. She's got trouble written all over her puss if you ask me."

"I was kind of hoping we could ask her..." Bert said.

Ada tossed off the lumbago medicine and grimaced as the stuff hit home.

"Well, don't look at me," she said. "The next time I see her I will break her skinny neck."

"What'd I tell you?" I said to Bert. "Women hate her and men turn into mush around her. There's no way we can interview her."

"How about by phone?" he said. "That way you wouldn't have to look at her."

"Hmm," I said, "might work. Ada, try the hotel, see if she'll come to the phone."

Ada grumbled but punched in the numbers and handed the phone to me.

"Hello? Grogan here. Look, will you see if the Rolls-

Royce woman will take a call from...? She doesn't? You sure? Yeah, okay." I hung up and turned to Bert. "She hasn't got a phone. She had it taken out. She values her privacy, he says."

"So that's that, then," Bert said. "The biggest story to hit this town in years and we can't get a word out of the leading lady."

"Maybe there's no story there after all," I said. "Who knows, she's probably just some dame who sells ladies' hosiery in Cleveland or something and is on her way to visit her old mother upstate somewhere."

Bert and Ada looked at me like I'd lost my senses and I shrugged. What the hell did I know?

The next day proved Bert right, though; the first casualty turned up and Midvale entered a fierce struggle for its very existence, a struggle that would divide the town and strain relations among families, friends, and passers-by.

It would also involve the rest of the world before it was over.

CHAPTER FIVE

First Casualty

The first one to go was Bill Swigert over at the florist shop. Bill was just an average Joe, had a wife and two grown kids and had run his shop across the street from the hotel for more than twenty years. He was an Elk and went to church every Sunday he couldn't get out of it and would have been completely at home on a Norman Rockwell magazine cover.

And then on the night of the third day after the Rolls-Royce woman showed up Bill closed his shop at six as usual and left with a delivery on his way home. He still hadn't arrived by eight the next morning and Mrs. Swigert called Chief Hawes to report him missing.

Bill wasn't missing long, though. At nine o'clock he was in Lola's having breakfast and wearing an odd, lopsided kind of grin that made him look just a little crazy. I happened by there for coffee and a cruller about 9:10 and saw him myself. He was sitting at the counter with a plate of scrambled eggs and his lopsided grin. Nobody knew then that he'd been missing all night so no one said anything special to him, but everybody noticed his wacky look.

What's more, he apparently wasn't his old self. Normally a mild mannered guy and even a little on the shy side, Bill was leering at every sexy woman in range. It's true he wouldn't tax his vision leering at pretty women in Lola's, but he leered at what was there.

For example, he sat where Mona the waitress had to bend a lot to fill orders and she was wearing a top that gaped a good bit when she leaned over.

Even worse, Mona had neglected to wear a bra and her excellent boobs swung free and thumped audibly together like a pair of ripe melons. Every time Mona leaned over Bill would lean over himself and look all the way down to the tops of Mona's shoes. And then he'd look around and grin that crazy grin and shove some more scrambled eggs into his mush.

About ten minutes later Chief Hawes came in and spotted him. He went up to Bill and said, "Bill, where you been? Your wife reported you missing."

Bill just looked at the Chief and grinned and Hawes was so taken aback he recoiled slightly and frowned.

"You okay, Bill?" he said. Bill just grinned and the Chief looked around for help and saw Kaz Mitchell, the pharmacist, sitting near the jukebox and motioned for him to come over.

Chief Hawes stopped Kaz a couple of feet away and said, "Kaz, somethin's wrong with Bill here. Look at him, he's not acting normal."

"Has he been hurt?" Kaz said. "Any bumps or bruises on him?"

"He looks okay to me. It's just he won't talk and he keeps smilin' like he's not all there."

Kaz went up to Bill and said, "Say, Bill, everything okay? You all right?"

More grinning. Kaz looked at the Chief and shrugged. Chief Hawes stepped up and took Bill by the arm.

"Hey, Bill, you better come with me," he said. "Your wife's worried about you. Come on, let's go on over to the station and let her know you're all right."

Bill obligingly put down his fork and accompanied the Chief from Lola's without comment. He did take one last look down Mona's blouse as he stood to leave, though.

I thought there might be a story there somewhere so I gulped the rest of my coffee and followed them out. We got to the police station and the Chief put Bill in his own office and called Doc Gramble. Since things are pretty informal around the station, I was able to talk to Bill for a minute or two but he still had nothing to say. He just went on grinning happily and eyeing a pinup calendar on the wall.

Doc Gramble got there and spent about ten minutes going over Bill to determine what if any trauma he might have suffered and came away empty-handed.

"There's nothing wrong with him that I can see," he said, "at least nothing physical. No wounds, nothing broken."

"But somethin's happened to him," Chief Hawes said. "Look at him. He won't talk and he can't get that silly grin off his face."

Doc shrugged and said, "Take him over to the hospital and let the psycho unit have a gander at him. Looks like it's all in his head."

So that's what they did and that was the end of it for a couple of days.

Nobody was alarmed, nobody suspected anything. I did a little piece about how Bill was undergoing some tests and his wife ran the shop and life went on as before.

A couple of days later I ran into Doc Gramble on the street and asked him about Bill. Doc had been following it up more out of curiosity than anything else and he said, "Nobody knows what it is. He's fine, nothing wrong at all that they can see. He's talking now, seems normal enough, but he doesn't say anything about what happened that night."

"Is he well enough to go home?"

"I think so, except he's got this fixation with women, with sex."

"Sex?"

"Yeah, he leers at the nurses and pinches them when they pass and winks at them and makes suggestive remarks. It's like something went off in his head and brought out all these latent thoughts about sex."

"But I heard Bill was a Christian and arrow straight," I said. "If he was he sure as hell isn't now. Something happened to him that night, something bizarre, crazy, even, and now he's a little crazy himself."

"It looks that way," Doc said. "But we may never know what it was, at least not until Bill's able to tell us."

"If you find out anything, let me know, will you?"

"Sure, but don't hold your breath."

I dropped into Kaz's drugstore for a couple of cigars and Kaz was busy arranging the condom display in front of the pharmacy counter. He was standing there with a double fistful of rubbers and he shook his head.

"I don't know what the world's coming to, Grogan,"

he said. "Look at this. People used to come in here and whisper they wanted condoms and now we put them on display like lollipops and Ace bandages."

"Things change, Kaz," I said. "I knew rubber ads couldn't be far behind when they started running ads for feminine hygiene products during the dinner hour."

"Nothing's sacred anymore. Sex sells. That's all they care about, the old bottom line."

"Speaking of sex, you see any more of the Rolls-Royce woman?"

"No, she seems to lie low pretty much. She's bought some stuff here but she sends Hilda over for it. Hilda's one of the maids."

An old geezer named Ezra Halley was looking through a magazine with a scantily clad bosomy girl on the cover being pursued by space creatures and he cocked an ear and moved a step in our direction, but I didn't pay him much attention because I was busy envisioning the Rolls-Royce woman lying low in a variety of interesting positions and sort of got caught up in it all.

"Grogan?" Kaz said.

"Hmmm?"

"Wake up. You've got that look in your eye again."

"Oh. Sorry. I was just thinking."

I trailed off absently and Kaz nodded and said, "Yeah. If I didn't know better, I'd think it was a hold-up."

I looked down and saw what he meant. "Jesus," I said, "and she isn't even here."

"She's here, all right," Kaz said ominously. "She's

got this town by the balls. Even when you can't see her you know she's up there, you can almost smell her. She's all people talk about now, the Rolls-Royce woman this and that, when somebody saw her last and what she was doing and what she wants and how long she's going to stay and where she came from and on and on."

"Okay, where did she come from?"

Ezra dropped his space mag and said, "She came from outer space, that's where she came from."

I looked at him. "Outer space?"

"Damn right," he said. "I saw it myself. A spaceship. Big as a train, it was. Landed in my pasture last week. She drove that white car of hers right out of that ship an' straight off my farm."

"This is Ezra Halley," Kaz said. "Ezra sees a lot of spaceships. They use his pasture for a landing strip six or seven times a year."

"Damn right they do," Ezra said. "We're bein' invaded by space aliens who look just like her. They're takin' over the country. Soon's they get in power they're gonna turn us all into love slaves an' make us do their biddin.'"

"If the aliens look like her, we're doomed," I said. "Every man in Midvale is under her spell. All she has to do is show up and we turn into love slaves on the spot."

"You keep an eye out, Ezra," Kaz said. "If you see any more spaceships in your pasture you let us know."

"Oh, there'll be some more, all right," Ezra said. "They come right regular." He looked farmward apprehensively. "Maybe I better go take a look. There might be one landin' right now."

He hurried off and Kaz said drily, "It wouldn't surprise me any."

"What's with Ezra? He the local loony?"

"Oh, he's harmless. He reads all the creatures from outer space magazines and gets carried away sometimes. He reports spaceships every once in a while and Bert writes them up for a little local color, but nobody takes him seriously."

"Who knows? Maybe he's right. We sure as hell don't know where the lady comes from."

"Maybe not but I'm pretty sure it's not from outer space," Kaz said. "That supernatural stuff is bunk. There aren't any ghosts or space creatures, it's all got a logical explanation behind it."

"Oh, yeah? Then explain how she raises dicks from the dead and turns strong men into quivering jelly just on her looks alone. You have to admit there's something spooky about it."

"Maybe she's just extra sexy."

"Maybe. And maybe every guy in Midvale is just extra horny lately."

I started to go and Kaz said, "How's Bill Swigert doing? They ever find out what's wrong with him?"

"Nope, still a mystery."

"Some folks say she did it, you know."

"Who?"

"The Rolls-Royce woman. They say she did something to him."

"What'd she do? And when? And how? Bill never even mentioned her."

Kaz shrugged. "I don't know. I'm just telling you what some people are saying. Maybe it's true, maybe not."

"What, do they think she's a witch or something? The next thing you know these half-wits will be sending for a rope. Somebody better tell Chief Hawes so he can keep an eye on 'em. If we aren't careful, we'll have Arthur Miller's ghost hanging around town doing research on another play."

"Oh, we don't lynch witches around here. Still, it might be a good idea to alert the Chief."

"I'll tell him. See you later, Kaz."

"Right."

He sighed heavily and began straightening stacks of condoms labeled lubricated with extra reservoirs and I bit the end off a cigar as I headed for the Beacon, but I found myself thinking about what Kaz said. What if she was involved in Bill's odd ailment? Maybe there was something more to all this than meets the eye.

CHAPTER SIX

Another Casualty And Plan A

The next day Midvale had its second victim. Horace Wahl, a farm equipment salesman, was found sitting on the curb at two a.m. with the same sappy grin Bill had worn. Officer Wally Hicks was on his rounds when he saw Horace and he asked him if he was all right but got no answer. Horace apparently couldn't—or wouldn't— talk, and Wally hauled him on over to the station and called Chief Hawes and the Chief told him to take Horace to the hospital.

The next morning the Chief called the Beacon and told me about Horace and I called Doc Gramble and then went to the hospital. Horace was happily watching TV, one of those music video things full of sexy, half-naked girls with great boobs dancing and gyrating all over the place. The shrink, Dr. Bane, met Doc Gramble and me in his office.

"I've never seen anything quite like it before," Dr. Bane said. "No sign of any injury, no abnormal vital signs, yet an apparent loss of speech, an odd smile, and an unusual interest in things erotic. It's almost like both men are under some kind of spell or something."

"How about drugs?" Doc said. "Could they have taken something? Maybe one of those newfangled designer drugs they're coming out with lately. We don't know how some of these might affect a man, you know."

Dr. Bane shrugged and said, "They weren't drug users before so it's not likely, but we can't know for sure. Besides, there aren't any tests to determine if so-called designer drugs have been used."

"There's always voodoo," I said.

"Voodoo?" Doc said.

"What makes you say that?" Dr. Bane said.

"Hey, I was only kidding. Maybe it's magic or something, maybe they both just went crazy all of a sudden, who knows? It could even be some kind of voodoo, though, couldn't it?"

"It could be if there were such a thing," Dr. Bane said. "But, as scientists, I'm afraid we need more to go on than a set of bongo drums and some chicken entrails."

"It's not magic, it's science, Grogan," Doc said. "It's all logic and natural laws and knowledge; if there's an answer here, we'll find it through good science."

Of course they were right, anybody could see that, and yet I wasn't so sure somehow. It was entirely possible that something totally unscientific was happening in Midvale, some phenomenon that defied all the test tubes and computers out there. I didn't tell them that, though, since I didn't want to look like an ignoramus, but I resolved to look into it on my own.

Anyway, I got to talk to Bill for a few minutes and had better luck this time. He still wore traces of the slaphappy grin but he was talking now.

"How're you feeling, Bill?" I asked.

"Oh, I feel fine," he said. "Fine."

"Good. Uh, look, Bill, about the other night there.

You know, the night you didn't come home? Well, did you see anyone that night? Did you run into anyone?"

"Sure, I saw Wally."

"Officer Hicks?"

"Yeah."

"Where?"

"On Main Street. In front of the hotel."

"Anyone else?"

"Sure, lots of people. I saw Lola, Art Fazer, Mayor Eli. Lots of people."

"Did you see anyone else? Like a stranger maybe? Did you go somewhere with someone?"

Bill grinned lopsidedly and, looking past my shoulder, shot his eyebrows à la Groucho and leered lewdly. I turned to look and saw a sexy young nurse bending down on one knee and exposing a whole lot of leg in the process while she adjusted the height of the bed opposite us. I looked back and saw a gleam in Bill's eye that would have alarmed a tough-as-nails porn star who'd just finished shooting her one-hundredth XXX movie.

I tried a new tack. "Some dish, eh?"

"Yeah," he said, "I'd like to fix her wagon for her, by God."

"What makes you think her wagon needs fixing?"

"They all need fixing. And I'm the man for the job."

The nurse came over then and started fluffing his pillows.

"You okay, Mr. Swigert?" she said cheerily. "Here, just let me fluff your pillows for you…"

Bill grinned at her and reached out and put his right hand smack on her boob. The nurse was a real pro, though, and didn't bat an eye. She just took his hand and removed it and said, "Now, now, Mr. Swigert, you mustn't do that. Remember, you said you'd keep your hands to yourself."

Bill just grinned.

So there we were. Two guys similarly afflicted in a matter of days with a heretofore unknown ailment and no clue as to the why and how of it all. It was becoming a first-rate detective story and I don't even like the damn things.

When I left the hospital I went to the hotel and talked to the clerk on duty there. He was a young guy named Jimmy who went to school at State to study hotel management, whatever the hell that is. They'll give a guy a degree in anything nowadays.

Anyway, he wasn't much help.

"Yeah, I was on duty that night. From midnight till eight. I didn't see any of them. Not Bill, not Mr. Wahl, and not the lady in the suite. None of them came through here."

"Do you see the lady much?"

"Only once. The day she checked in."

"And?"

"You ever see her?"

"Yeah, I've seen her."

"Well?"

"Yeah, I know. You've never seen anything so sexy in your whole life."

Jimmy leaned his elbows on the counter and started to slip into a state I recognized all too well. "Yeah," he said dreamily, "she had the nicest boobs and hips that moved like a goddess crossing a moonlit street in high heels and..."

I knew where he was going so I left and stopped at Lola's for a cheeseburger and fries and met Ellen on her way out.

"You eat already?" I asked.

"Just finished. And I've got an appointment or I'd keep you company."

"Okay, look, how about a movie tonight?"

"I'd like to, Jack, but, well, I've already got plans."

"What? You mean I have a rival?"

"I don't know that rival's the right word," she said smiling, "but I do have a date."

"Okay. Maybe another time."

"Sure. Call me."

She left and I watched her go and found myself unconsciously thinking of a goddess crossing a street wearing high heels until Lola's voice snapped me back to reality.

"Hey, Grogan, are you comin' in or what? Make up your mind and close the door before the place fills up with flies."

I went in and scarfed down the burger and fries and eavesdropped on some farmers who were arguing whether the Rolls-Royce woman was responsible for the recent lack of rainfall. Christ, I thought, they'll be blaming her for falling farm prices and the loss of the ozone layer if they keep it up.

I went back to the Beacon and knocked out a story on Beulah Jones' new twin calves and Ralph Booker's new John Deere tractor and his plans to enter it in the

Saturday night tractor pull down at the fairgrounds and ended up sharing a tumbler full of bourbon with Art and Bert in the office.

The subject was, as usual lately, the Rolls-Royce woman and how we could finagle an interview without jeopardizing life and limb of the reporter.

"Maybe we could write her a letter," Art said. "She might answer some questions by mail."

"It's a long shot," I said.

"Give it a try, Art," Bert said. "What've we got to lose?"

"Maybe we could ask her to disguise herself," I said. "You know, wear frumpy clothes and dark glasses and no makeup and sensible shoes. She wouldn't be so sexy and we could keep our wits about us long enough to get the interview."

"Wouldn't work," Art said, shaking his head. "What would you do about the pheromones? One whiff and you'd be knocked senseless again."

"You're right. Boy, if you could only bottle that scent you'd corner the perfume market overnight."

"The whole town's talkin' about her," Bert said. "Most of them would give their eye teeth to know what the hell she's up to. We've got to figure a way to get that interview."

"You'll need a blind guy," I said.

"A blind man who can't smell, either," Art said.

"That's it!" Bert said. "If he can't see her or smell her, he'd be immune!"

"You actually know somebody like that?" I said.

"Yeah, you," Bert said.

"Me?"

"Sure. Look, all you need is dark glasses and some cotton stuffed up your nose. Ten minutes and you'll be out of there."

"I don't know," I said hesitantly. "I'm not sure..."

"Look, it'll work. Trust me. Art'll even go with you. He can wait outside."

"What the hell, why not?" I said. "It's only a woman, right? How threatening can one solitary woman be?"

"Maybe more'n we know," Art said ominously.

Anyway, it was decided. I got the darkest glasses Kaz had in stock at his drugstore and stuffed six or seven balls of cotton in my nose and headed for the hotel with Art tagging along for moral support.

Jimmy was still on duty at the desk.

"The Rolls-Royce woman in?" I asked.

"She must be," he said. "I didn't see her leave. Want me to ring her room?"

"Uh, no, that's okay. We'll just go on up."

We took the elevator to the sixth-floor and started down the hall when Willie the bellhop rounded the corner and came toward us. He was wearing the same wacky grin as the others and we knew right away the scourge had struck again.

I stopped Willie and said, "Willie! What's wrong? Are you all right?"

He just grinned happily and I saw a twinkle in his eye that I'd pay good money to see in my own. Art reached out to hold him and keep him from bouncing gently against the wall in a kind of blissful slow motion and said, "Just like the other two, knocked senseless."

"Okay, let's go have our interview."

"What about Willie?"

"Bring him along. He's okay. Hell, he's only seventeen, nothing can hurt a guy that young."

When we turned the corner we saw the door of a linen closet was standing open. I looked in and saw the piled sheets and pillowcases had been knocked to the floor and thrown about and trampled as though somebody had done something violent on them. I looked at Willie.

"Willie, were you in here? Were you in the linen closet a few minutes ago?"

He just grinned and bounced into the wall.

"So?" Art said.

"Beats me. Maybe..." I didn't finish the thought. "Come on, let's go."

We advanced to the door of room 666 and I rapped smartly on it. After a moment the door opened and I quickly slipped on the dark glasses. "Uh, is the lady of the house in?" I asked lamely when I suddenly realized I didn't even know her name.

"No," a voice said, "she went out. I'm Hilda."

I raised my glasses and peeked cautiously out like somebody checking to see if it's really Medusa and saw that it wasn't.

"Hi, I'm Grogan from the Beacon. Could I come in for a minute?"

"No, she told me not to let anyone in. I think I'd better do what she says."

"Can you tell me anything about her? You know, where'd she come from? Where's she going? How long is she going to...?"

Hilda shook her head. "She never tells me anything like that. All she says is do this or go there or be here at one o'clock." She shot nervous glances left and right and said, "But there's something strange about her, all right. She always looks perfect, her hair's never messed up and she's got a look in her..."

There was a sound of a door slamming in some distant part of the suite and Hilda looked over her shoulder and quickly shut the door in my face.

"She must be home, after all," Art said.

"Yeah, but I don't think Hilda knew it. She really looked surprised."

"So what now?"

"First, I take this goddam cotton out of my nose, we take Willie to the hospital, then we check with Chief Hawes. After that, who knows?"

And that's what we did.

CHAPTER SEVEN

Of Window Peepers And Wally's Near Miss

Dr. Bane shook his head. "I've never seen anything like it. Three men suffer major personality changes overnight, and there is no discernible reason. Amazing."

"A virus?" I said.

"I don't know what the hell it is. I thought maybe it had something to do with men in middle age since Swigert and Wahl are both around fifty, but then Willie comes down with it and he's only a seventeen-year-old kid. And he's got a bad case. Why, last night the head nurse caught him and one of the nurses in flagrante delicto in the linen closet. In flagrante delicto yet."

"A linen closet?"

"Yes, out in the ward. Then this morning he grabbed nurse Bailey's breasts in both hands and wouldn't let go. And this is a kid who won a blue ribbon in Sunday school just two weeks ago. I doubt if the kid ever entertained an erotic thought until last night and all of a sudden he's trying to get into the pants of every nurse in the place."

"What are you going to do?"

"What can I do? Nothing. I don't even know what the hell these guys have. I can't treat what I can't identify."

"How are Swigert and Wahl?"

"Fine. I sent them home. Except for getting erections every fifteen minutes and grinning like Cheshire cats, there's nothing wrong with them."

The rest of our conversation was just more of the same. I started for the Beacon and reflected on things. Somewhere in all this there was a story, maybe even a big story. Who knows? There might even be a Pulitzer for an enterprising reporter like myself. But what the hell was going on? There'd be no story until I found out.

Bert was on the phone when I got in but he motioned me into his office. He had Rev. Skaggs on the line. "Sure. On the back page. No problem. I've got the copy right here. Right, a quarter page. Okay." He hung up. "Rev. Skaggs just ordered a quarter-page ad for Thursday. He's holdin' a big meetin' on our friend across the street. Says something about her bein' the Devil's helper."

"The man's an idiot," I said.

"Maybe so, but he makes a lot of noise around this town. He could stir up mucho trouble."

"Just so he keeps buying ads."

"What about her?" Bert said. "Is she a devil?"

I shrugged. "I doubt it. Still..."

"Still what?"

"Well, Hilda, she's the maid, Hilda said she wasn't home when we got there and I don't think she was. I mean, when Hilda found out she was home she seemed really surprised. There's only one door to that suite so how could she be out and then return without Hilda seeing her?"

"Maybe she was in the back somewhere."

"Yeah, maybe."

"So. What about our interview?"

"What interview? The lady isn't talking. If we get a story, it'll have to be some other way."

"Okay, let's try a little window peeping," Bert said.

"Window peeping? Isn't that against the law?"

"So what? We're reporters, aren't we? Remember the reporter's creed: the story at any cost. Besides, you'll peep at long range. All you have to do is climb up on the City Hall tower across the street and spy on her with these binoculars."

He reached into a desk drawer and brought out a pair of heavy binoculars, the kind army tank commanders used in the war.

"One problem."

"What?"

"I won't do it."

"Why not?"

"Because it's crazy, that's why. For one thing, Tarzan himself couldn't climb that goddam tower without a hook and ladder truck, and for another what do I do if I spot her? You remember what happens to guys who get a look at her? Their minds snap and they can only think erotic and sensual thoughts about pudenda and boobs and creamy thighs and wild bursts of raw sexual energy and..."

Bert grabbed my lapels and gave me another good shaking and I snapped out of it.

"Easy, Grogan," he said, "you're going under again."

"Whew!" I said. Then, "There, that only proves

my point. If I go under like that while dangling eighty feet above the sidewalk with a twenty-pound pair of binoculars around my neck and a hard-on the size of a Louisville slugger..."

"A what?"

"All right, a billy club then." Bert raised a quizzical eyebrow and I said, "Okay, okay, so maybe a billy club is stretching it a bit but..."

"Okay, you made your point," he said. He thought for a minute, then, "Hey, how about if you climb down the fire escape from the roof and spy on her from there? At least you wouldn't have to worry about fallin.'"

"Look, forget this window-peeping business. I'd probably end up in jail as a Peeping Tom and how would that look?" I drew an imaginary headline in the air. "'Beacon Reporter Arrested As Peeping Tom.' Shit. Rev. Skaggs'd have a ball with that one."

Bert sighed and said, "Yeah, I guess you're right. But I hate to miss out on a good story, and any copyboy would know there's a story there somewhere."

"I'll keep an eye on her, or at least on her immediate vicinity, and something may come up."

"Okay, that'll have to do, I guess."

More wasted effort. I went back to my desk and put the finishing touches on another report of spaceships seen in Ezra's pasture. This time he claimed they made off with some of his cows and he had the hoof prints that showed right where they were standing when abducted as proof. He wanted to know if I thought Orson Welles might be interested in buying the rights and I didn't have the heart to tell him Orson's dead.

Such was journalism in Midvale but I couldn't

complain. Hell, I was humming right along on my novel and would soon have the introduction nicely out of the way. I expected to start the first chapter no later than Labor Day, and would have, too, if only there weren't so much labor involved in the whole process.

Anyway, I took Ellen to the Bijou that night and we had dinner at Woo's Pagoda on Maple and, like everybody else, we talked about the Rolls-Royce woman.

"I saw her yesterday," Ellen said. "On Main Street. She was coming out of Kaz's drugstore."

"And?"

"And I don't like her."

"Why not?"

"Because she's a tramp."

"A tramp? Come on, this is the 21st century, for God's sake. We don't call women tramps anymore."

"I know that," she said, "but I mean tramp in the best sense in that she's the type who'll pursue any man, married or engaged or what have you. It's written all over her; she's every woman's arch enemy."

"Aha, then you're jealous of her. That's why all the women hate her so much, because she's a threat to the rest of you."

"Maybe."

"Sure, that's it! She's a hussy, a vamp, a Jezebel..."

"And that's why all the men are attracted to her, isn't it?" she said. "Because men like amoral women, sexpots who flaunt their sexuality and brazenly offer themselves as sex objects."

"Yeah," I said, visions of the Rolls-Royce woman offering herself beginning to do unheard of things to my libido again. Fortunately, the waitress showed up then and asked if we wanted more plum wine and snapped me out of my reverie.

"Do you find her sexy?" Ellen asked after our glasses had been refilled.

"I'd be lying if I denied it," I said. "The woman exudes sexuality from every pore. You saw it for yourself. When you saw her yesterday what were all the guys doing? Standing around with their mouths open, that's what. She could have her pick of the lot with a nod of her head or the wink of an eye. I'd have to say that's sexy, wouldn't you?"

Ellen picked up her wine and looked at me over the rim of her glass as she prepared to drink. "And do you find me sexy, too?"

"As a matter of fact, I do," I said.

"Good. Let's go back to your place."

And we did, or we started to, anyway, but we never got any further than the hotel when we ran into Chief Hawes who was on his way out. He saw me and said, "Hey, Grogan, got something here you'll be interested in."

"Well, I'm in a bit of a hurry right now, Chief..." I started to say but he interrupted me.

"Got two more," he said. "Jimmy the desk clerk and Toby Cruickshank from Asa's hardware. Both goners just like the others."

"Holy shit!" I said. "It's a goddam epidemic!"

"There's more," the Chief said, "Wally Hicks is over at the hospital. Found him wandering around behind Kaz's place. He wasn't wearing any pants."

"No pants?"

"What happened to his pants?" Ellen asked.

"Don't know. He says he can't remember. The last thing he knew he was making his rounds and he saw something or smelled something and he got kind of dizzy and then Nick from Andy's found him sittin' on a packing case behind Kaz's drugstore."

"But he can talk?" I said. "He's not zonked out like the rest of them?"

"No, he's okay, but he's got a gleam in his eye like they had and he's kind of screwed-up."

"She did it," Ellen said firmly.

"Who?" the Chief said.

"The Rolls-Royce woman."

"Wait a minute," I said, "you don't know that. You just don't like her, you said so yourself."

"You're right, I don't like her, but that's beside the point. I say that woman had something to do with it. She's putting a hex on people."

"You can't charge a woman in court with hexing people," Hawes said.

"Say, where was Wally earlier?" I said. "Was he at the hotel?"

Hawes shrugged. "He must've been, it's on his beat. He covers downtown and that includes the hotel."

"And Jimmy was at the hotel," Ellen said.

"And so was Wahl, he was staying there," I said.

"And I'll bet Bill Swigert and Toby Cruickshank were in that hotel, too," Ellen said. "And that's where that woman is!"

"Ellen's got a point there, Chief," I said. "If all those guys were at the hotel, she's got to be involved somehow."

"Let's go talk to Wally again," the Chief said. "Maybe we can jog his memory."

I looked at Ellen and she looked at me. "Well," I said, "we were..."

"Oh, go ahead, Jack," Ellen said. "We'll have lunch tomorrow and you can tell me what you found out."

"Okay," I said, "Lola's at noon."

She smiled and I repaired to the hospital with Chief Hawes where we found Wally with his nose buried in a copy of Penthouse and a half-sappy grin on his face. He looked up when we came in.

"How's it goin,' Wally?" the Chief said.

Wally shook his head and said, "Okay, I guess." He looked around vacantly. "You find my pants yet?"

"Not yet."

"You all right, Wally?" I asked.

"Yeah, I think so," he said uncertainly. "'Cept I can't find my pants."

"Maybe you left them over at the hotel," the Chief said.

Wally shook his head again and stole a look at the centerfold in his lap and then looked up. "I don't think so but I'm not sure..."

"You were at Andy's pool hall at nine and you had your pants on then," Hawes said. "A half-hour later you were pant-less at Kaz's place. Did you go by the hotel after you left Andy's?"

Wally looked blankly at Hawes and then back to the centerfold and he grinned the sappy grin again. Hawes looked at me and shrugged. We left and ran into Dr. Bane in the hall.

"What's with Wally, Doc?" I said. "Is he another

one or...?"

"I only saw him for a few minutes," Dr. Bane said, "but offhand I'd say he had a close call. Whatever happened to the others probably happened to him, too, but somehow he got away with less of a jolt. His memory's a little off and he's been studying that Penthouse like he's never seen a naked lady before, but he's not as bad as the others. I think he can go home tomorrow."

"How about Jimmy and Cruickshank?"

"They're pretty wobbly but they'll be okay. Whatever it is, it doesn't last long except for the personality change. That may even be permanent."

"You mean they'll be hooked on erotic stuff forever?" the Chief said.

Dr. Bane nodded. "They seem to become more sensual, more interested in physical gratification than they were before. They sort of fall into a kind of hedonism, especially sexually. They'll probably be lifelong subscribers to Playboy."

"But still no idea how they got that way?" I said.

"Not a one. Maybe it's a virus or something, or maybe it's some kind of hysteria, but whatever it is it's a new one on me."

"Sounds like there might be an article for the medical journal here somewhere, Doc," I said.

"I was thinking that myself," Dr. Bane said. "Strangest thing I've ever seen. Almost like there's something supernatural, almost..." He trailed off and started down the hall.

I turned to the Chief. "Let's go see if we can find Wally's pants."

"Where you gonna look?"

"We'll start with the hotel. If Wally was at the hotel, and if all the others were, too, maybe there's something going on over there that we need to look into."

"You mean the Rolls-Royce woman?"

"Could be."

We left the hospital and headed for the hotel. Once there we talked to various people who might have seen Wally or Cruickshank earlier that night and we struck pay dirt right away. One of the cooks had given Wally a cup of coffee a little after nine but didn't know where else he went in the hotel or when he left. It wasn't much but at least it placed Wally in the hotel.

"So we know for a fact they were all in the hotel except Swigert and Cruickshank," Hawes said.

"And I'll bet they were, too," I said. "And that means whatever happened to them most likely happened somewhere in the hotel—and it probably had something to do with the lady in 666."

"Come on, let's look the place over. Maybe we can find Wally's pants for him."

We left the kitchen and the Chief began conducting a cursory search of the various closets and storage rooms we passed. He opened one door and started to close it, then did a double take and looked again. "Hey, look at this, Grogan," he said.

I looked over his shoulder and there were sacks of flour and whey and whatnot surrounded by a lot of empty lard buckets that had fallen down and were all over the room. And there on a pile of empty gunnysacks I saw Wally's pants.

"Wally's pants," I said.

"Yeah, but what the hell are they doin' in here?"

"Depends. What was Wally doing in here?"

"And who was he doin' it with?"

"You know damn well who."

"So? Now what? It's all guess work, we got no real evidence."

"So you're the cop, get some evidence. Stake the place out, go undercover, bug it, pay informers, re-enact the crime. How do you usually catch people like her?"

"Why ask me? I've never even seen anybody like her before."

"My guess is that she's your man," I said. "It's too coincidental for my money. She shows up and all of a sudden guys who haven't thought about sex in years are coming up with foot-long donnikers and leering at every woman in sight. She moves into the Midvale Manor and it looks like all the guys afflicted were in there at one time or another, too. It's an open and shut case."

"Okay, I'll put some undercover guys on her," the Chief said. "Keep her under surveillance. Maybe we can catch her in the act, get some pictures or something. If she's the one who's fuckin' these guys up, we'll find it out soon enough."

Or would we?

CHAPTER EIGHT

Rev. Skaggs Is Routed—And So Am I

The next day was Thursday and I had lunch with Ellen as planned and brought her up to date on our mysterious friend.

"She's the one, all right," I said. "I'd stake my reputation on it."

"I knew it," Ellen said. "Every woman knows she's guilty because..."

She stopped and I looked at her. "Because every woman sees a little of herself in her. Isn't that what you were going to say?"

"No, I was going to say we...it's instinct, that's all. Call it women's intuition or just a feeling, but there's evil written all over her."

"I don't know anything about evil, but she's got to be the one who's doing in our local citizenry," I said. "But what the hell is she doing?"

"Maybe it's drugs of some kind."

"Yeah, that's my guess, too, but what drugs? I never heard of a drug turning people into sex maniacs overnight, did you?"

"No, not really."

"Boy, I hope it's something sensational," I said. "Maybe black magic. It could even be voodoo. You got any Brazilians living in Midvale? You know, people who buy a lot of live chickens and beat drums all night?"

She shook her head. "We had some Gypsies once, but they just played violins and danced around campfires. I don't remember any drums."

"Well, whatever it is, I've got a feeling I'm going to get one dandy story out of all this before I'm done here. And if there's any black magic, I may end up on the cover of Time."

"But first you have to find out what's really going on."

"Yeah, and how am I going to do it? I need a plan."

Ellen looked at her watch. "Oh, I've got to get back. I'm taking a client out to see the Hopworth place this afternoon."

"Well, uh, you want to try again tonight?" I said. "My place?"

She smiled. "Sure, why not?"

"Good. About eight?"

"I'll be there."

She left and I paid the check and went back to the Beacon where Bert was going over the day's printing in his office with Tom. I slipped on by and banged out a story of how Ed Skeet's beaver dam broke and flooded McSwain's back forty and nearly drowned out his entire peanut crop.

It was Dullsville all the way so I lightened it up a bit by implying a band of Save the Beavers activists had been alerted and would investigate to learn if anyone had blown the dam in an effort to harm the furry denizens of the pond. What the hell, it might even have been true. There are bands out there trying to save everything from whales to ozone, so why not beavers?

I'd no sooner finished up when Bert came back and said, "Skaggs is holding his meeting tonight, Grogan. You cover it. Eight sharp at the tent over on Spruce."

"Tonight?" I said. "I had plans for tonight."

"Cancel them. We've gotta keep an eye on Skaggs or he'll stir those half-wits up and do something crazy."

"All right, all right, I'll go but my heart's not in it."

"I don't want your heart, just a story. Remember, the fun starts at eight sharp."

I called Ellen and canceled again. She sounded a little pissed but what could I do? That night I walked over to Spruce and found the parking lot half-full of pickups and Jeeps. There was a new Mercedes parked near the entrance so I knew Skaggs was already inside. People wearing baseball caps and polyester sport coats were streaming in with expectant looks on their faces and recorded organ music filled the night air. I trudged in behind the faithful and took up a spot down front where I lounged against a tent pole and surveyed the crowd.

At eight sharp Skaggs walked out on the stage and started an oration about evil forces in Midvale and the Devil's work and how good Christians had a responsibility to protect themselves and their children from immorality and whatnot. Then he announced a collection and his aides sent large wicker baskets through the crowds and they were quickly filled to overflowing with bills and promissory notes.

Then he turned to the business at hand.

"We have a strange—and I think an evil—presence

in Midvale," he said. "There is a certain woman in our midst, a woman with sinister powers who puts evil thoughts in men's minds and seduces them in mysterious ways. This woman goes out on our very streets and fills the air with sensuality, she fills the air with lustfulness, she fills the air with visions of raw SEX!"

There was an audible gasp from the women in the crowd while the men stared forward fixedly and licked parched lips and breathed through slightly opened mouths.

"This woman is staying at the Midvale Manor at this very moment," Skaggs went on. "She dresses provocatively and moves seductively and looks at men with eyes that offer a universal challenge and she dares them to accept her challenge." He lowered his voice and leaned closer. "I have seen this woman myself. She has strong, nearly irresistible powers; there is a mocking in her smile, pride in her eyes; I tell you, she's an evil force sent to Midvale to destroy us with her unbridled sexuality, and I say that woman was sent here by Satan himself!"

The crowd went nuts. Women demanded she be driven out of town while the men stared and licked their lips and the aides scurried around with the wicker baskets again to take advantage of the moment and rake in another collection before anyone realized they'd already had one.

Well, after a few minutes a hush suddenly fell over the place and everyone turned and craned his neck to see what the hell was going on and there was the Rolls-Royce woman coming down the main aisle. Women drew back and hissed and bared their teeth at the sight of her and their men let their jaws drop even as certain other things rose and they gaped in blissful awe at the sight.

A lot of what happened is a little vague now because I was also gaping and rising with all the rest, but I do remember that she advanced to the front of the tent and turned and looked at the crowd and then she laughed. It wasn't a loud laugh, though; in fact, it was the smallest of laughs, but the sound of it struck terror into every woman's heart even as it penetrated every male libido and drove them all wild.

Skaggs himself followed in the direction pointed by his own wildly erect donniker and leapt from the stage and into the crowd in an effort to get at the "evil force" before him. Everybody rose as one and the women hissed like a lot of pissed-off snakes and the men ran in circles and clutched frantically at assorted boobs and thighs and keisters that came their way. The next thing I knew I was outside on the sidewalk and Chief Hawes was there with several cops who struggled to gain control of what had turned out to be a mini-riot.

The Rolls-Royce woman was nowhere to be seen by then, though, and I finally regained my wits and went off to Brady's to steady my nerves with a double Scotch. I ordered my drink and the mayor called me from a nearby table.

"Hey, Grogan," he said. "Come on, sit over here."

He and Carl Parks were sharing a pitcher of beer and a bowl of peanuts and I joined them.

"What's new, Grogan?" Carl said.

"For once I think I've got a scoop," I said. "I just

came from Rev. Skaggs' meeting. Ended up with a full-scale riot."

"A riot?" Eli said.

"He was maligning the Rolls-Royce woman and had the crowd whipped into a near frenzy when she walked in and laughed in their goddam faces. Place went berserk. All the women were enraged and wanted to scratch her eyes out and all the guys had hard-ons and wanted to fuck her brains out."

"No shit!" Carl said.

"Why, that hussy!" Eli said. "I wish I'd a been there, by God! I'd a showed her a thing or two!"

"Somehow I don't think so, Eli," I said. "I don't think anybody shows that lady anything."

"It's a job for Chief Hawes, if you ask me," Carl said. "If the woman's a public nuisance, he oughta bring charges against her. If he hauls her into court, maybe we can get some kind of restraining order on her."

I took a good hit of Scotch and came to a decision of my own. "I want the story first," I said. "The more I see of her the more I'm convinced there's a whopping good story in here somewhere and I want it. And I'm going to get it." I finished off my drink and started up.

"Where you goin'?" Eli said.

"I'm a reporter; I'm going to get the story."

I left the bar and headed across the street to the hotel. I went in and through the lobby and out to the kitchen. It was after nine and the place was empty except for Mavis, a woman who worked in the kitchen. She was cleaning some kettles near the back door and didn't hear me.

I wandered around through the kitchen area and out into the hall and opened the door where the Chief and I had found Wally's pants. I looked in and saw the same sacks on the floor and the stacks of lard buckets that had been restacked in tall columns. I went in and studied the room as though looking for some sense in all this when suddenly I sensed—or maybe smelled—the presence of someone else in the room. I looked over my shoulder and my heart leapt into my throat and I instantly had the granddaddy of all hard-ons.

The Rolls-Royce woman was standing between me and the door and she was sex personified in a thin silken gown that hung open from floor to chin and revealed spectacular boobs and lots of white skin and a pudendum that was at once all pudenda and the only one. A great rush of heat engulfed me and I felt myself moving toward this incredible creature as she moved to meet me. I gazed into her laughing eyes and reached out and then I was sitting on the floor amidst an ocean of lard buckets and Mavis was bending over me.

"You okay, mister?" she said.

"Huh? What?"

"What you doin' in here anyway? I jus' pick up all these buckets yesterday an' now I gotta do it agin.'"

"Where'd she go?" I said, looking around.

"Where'd who go? Ain't nobody in here but us."

"The Rolls-Royce woman. She was just in here. Didn't you see her?"

"I ain't seen nothin'. All I know is I heard somebody kickin' these buckets aroun' agin' and I come in here and fin' you."

This time it hit me. "Again?"

"Yeah. That cop was kickin' them aroun' las' night."

So that's how Wally and I escaped! We both knocked over the buckets and the noise interrupted her before she could work us over. I struggled to my feet and took inventory to make sure everything was where it should be and beat a hasty retreat back to Brady's where I had another double Scotch before going home and crawling into bed.

I slept not well but long, and dreamed of naked women with five-hundred-pound boobs and cavernous pudenda and laughing eyes.

CHAPTER NINE

The Rolls-Royce Woman Identified; Plan B Flops

The next day I went out to the hospital to see how some of the victims from the Skaggs disaster were doing and I met Doc Gramble in the parking lot.

"Morning, Doc. Anything new?"

"Dr. Bane called. Said he thinks he's found something."

"He has, eh? I hope it's something sensational."

"If it isn't, you'll make it sensational, anyway."

"We've got to sell papers, Doc," I said. He growled something inaudible and we proceeded into the hospital and into Dr. Bane's office. A guy I recognized as one of Skaggs' aides was watching an X-rated video on TV and he wore the by now familiar goofy look shared by all the victims.

"Gentlemen," Dr. Bane said, "I now know what ails the victims of this strange malady." He pointed dramatically at his patient and said, "Careful analysis of brain waves reveals that this poor devil has had his brains fucked out!"

"What!" Doc Gramble said.

"Impossible!"

"No, it's true. Look at this man. He's got the I.Q. of a field mouse."

"So what?" I said. "He was Skaggs' aide. It's

probably genetic."

"No, I've checked four other victims and they're all the same. No brains. It's an exceedingly rare condition, one usually found only in medical literature and apparently not uncommon in the Middle Ages. The victims seem to be associated with some sort of unusual sexual activity, a fact that played a role in naming the condition. It's known as the Fucked Brainless Syndrome."

"But that's just an expression, nobody actually ever gets his brains fucked out," I said. "Besides, people can't live sans brains. How would a man function without a brain?"

"Oh, they still have brains, all right, it's just that they've suffered some trauma to the cerebellum," Dr. Bane said, "the part of the brain that controls sensual things. They're normal in most ways but they have this obsession with sex and erotica and they tend to hedonism."

"And?"

"And nothing," Doc Gramble said. "That's all anybody knows about it. I've not even heard the condition mentioned since medical school."

"Jesus, what a story!" I said. "A strange woman comes to town and fucks men's brains out! This one has Pulitzer written all over it!"

"Not so fast, Grogan," Dr. Bane said. "We better go slow here. We don't want to cause a panic. I think we should hold off publicizing this until we get some idea of where we're heading with it."

"Jim's right," Doc Gramble said, "it's better to err on the side of caution. Keep it under your hat for twenty-four hours, Grogan."

"But...!"

"We have to be responsible, Grogan, we owe it to people," Dr. Bane said.

"Okay, okay, one day," I said. "But I can't wait until tomorrow."

I went back to the Beacon and had to bite my tongue all day. It was all I could do to keep from running down Main Street like a modern Paul Revere warning people that their brains were at risk. I went to lunch at Lola's and talked to people and feigned interest in what they were saying, but I was really more intent on composing tomorrow's headlines.

After lunch I took a stroll around town while enjoying a cigar and all of a sudden I had a thought that stopped me in my tracks. An ailment out of the Middle Ages? Wasn't that a time when...?

I turned on my heel and made for the town library. Once arrived there, I dug through the card catalogues without being sure what the hell I was looking for and an hour later sat surrounded by books on the occult and spirits and what have you. I remembered something I'd read or heard about mythical sex creatures and demons and nightmares and I finally found it. Succubus! That was it. I knew I had my answer even before I read the words. It was perfect; it just made perfect sense and explained everything. I scanned the page with bated breath.

SUCCUBUS, (pl. succubi) a lascivious female demon from the Middle Ages said to possess sleeping men in sexual intercourse...

INCUBUS, (pl. incubi) its male counterpart.

According to one legend, they were said to be fallen angels who followed Lucifer when he was cast from Heaven...

We were dealing with a goddam succubus! I scrapped my promise to keep it quiet because a succubus is real news and no reporter sits on real news, at least not the kind that can shock the world. I slammed the book closed and rushed over to the police station where Chief Hawes was busy going over the week's crime reports, a job that took all of ten minutes since crime wasn't all that common in Midvale.

"Chief, I found the answer!" I said. "I know what she is!"

"What who is?" he said, looking up.

"The Rolls-Royce woman, she's a goddam succubus!"

"A goddam what?"

"A succubus, a demon who fucks guys' brains out. That's what she did to Swigert and all the rest of them. She caught them alone somewhere and fucked them and it scrambled their brains."

"Grogan, you can't fuck a man's brains out..."

"Oh, yeah? Tell that to Doc Bane. He ran some brain wave tests on the Rolls-Royce woman's victims and found out they're suffering from the Fucked Brainless Syndrome."

"Doc Bane said that?"

"Damn right he did. He said it appeared in medical literature in the Middle Ages and I remembered succubi were popular then so I looked them up and there she was. She's a goddam succubus, I tell you."

"Demons aren't real, Grogan," he said. "What am I

supposed to do, arrest a demon? How would that look in court? 'Your Honor, I charge this woman with being a demon who fucks men's brains out.' Gimme a break, will ya?"

"But it's true," I said. "I know, she almost got me last night."

"What? You saw her last night?"

"Yeah, at the hotel. I knew she was at the bottom of all this and I decided to track her down myself. I went to the hotel and looked in the room where we found Wally's pants and the next thing I knew she was in there with me. Christ, she was gorgeous and she had this kind of see-through gown on and the most fabulous tits I've ever seen. I guess I got hypnotized or something because I was completely helpless and then I came to and I was lying in a bunch of lard buckets and Mavis was helping me up."

"Mavis?"

"Yeah, she works in the kitchen—and she was the one who found Wally. That's how he and I escaped with our brains intact. We both knocked over those lard buckets and Mavis heard the noise. When she came in the Rolls-Royce woman took off. If it hadn't been for Mavis, Wally and I'd be grinning idiots memorizing centerfolds like the rest of them."

"Jesus, what if she really is a demon?" he said.

"What do you mean, if? I just told you she's a demon. I looked it up, for God's sake."

Hawes scratched his head. "So what do we do about it? We don't have any laws against demons."

"You better come up with something before she fucks every guy in Midvale and turns us all into a bunch of grinning sex maniacs," I said. "We're dealing with a crisis here, the future of the town's at stake."

"Okay, let's get Carl and Eli in here and see if they've got any ideas. If you're right about her, we're gonna need a lot of help." He reached for the phone.

"I say send for the Marines."

"Shit, I never even saw a demon before." Then, into the phone. "Eli? Can you come on down for a minute? We've got a little problem here. Yeah." He punched in new numbers. "Carl? Come on in here for a minute, will ya? Right."

"Now we're getting somewhere," I said. "We'll have her on her way out of town by nightfall, by God!"

Eli and Carl came in and I told them my story. At first they were incredulous, but I convinced them I knew what I was talking about and when I finished everybody sat back and looked at each other.

"So arrest her ass," Eli said at last.

"On what grounds?" Hawes said.

"Soliciting a police officer," Eli said.

"But she didn't solicit a police officer," Hawes said.

"Not yet she hasn't, but she will," Eli said. "Send a cop over there and she'll try to fuck his brains out, right? Well, as soon as she makes her move, bam! he slaps the cuffs on her."

Hawes looked at me and I shrugged. What the hell did I know?

"It'd be legal," Carl said. "Accosting and soliciting is a crime in Midvale."

"Okay," Hawes said, "let's try it. I'll need a volunteer, though. Can't order a man to take a chance on gettin' his brains fucked out, you know."

And so the Chief called the force together that very afternoon in the squad room and laid the plan on them.

"Men," he said, "I need a volunteer. It's dangerous work, maybe real dangerous. We've got us a real live succubus, the most beautiful and sexy woman in the whole world, and she specializes in fuckin' men's brains out." A murmur swept the ranks. "I need a man with the balls to face her down, a real man who can stand up tall and look her in the eye and let her know who's in charge!"

Each man stood just a little taller and looked at his neighbor with just the hint of a sneer on his lips and a macho glint in his eye.

"Okay, here's the plan," Hawes continued. "This woman tries to lay every guy she sees, so when we send a cop to her room she'll try to nail him and when she does bam! he slaps the cuffs on her and arrests her for accosting and soliciting. That's it. Now, who'll give it a shot?"

The men looked at each other for a moment, then Tommy Boyle stepped forward. Tommy was six-four and weighed over two hundred pounds and was said to have a donniker like a long, fat salami. "I'll do it, Chief," he said. "They don't make 'em too sexy for me."

His colleagues called out supportive remarks such as, "You tell them, Tommy!" and "Show 'er what a real man can do!" and "Make her cry uncle, Tommy!" and so on.

Chief Hawes beamed. "'Atta boy, Tommy," he said.

"I knew you guys wouldn't let the department down." He put an affectionate arm around Boyle's shoulders. "Now remember, you go in and say it's police business. She'll turn on the charm and when she does bam! you cuff her. Got that?"

Tommy grinned. "Got it," he said. He waved to the others and strode purposefully from the room and out of the station and over to the hotel. The entire department followed at a distance of some yards and watched as he entered the front door of the hotel. They stood about in small groups eyeing the door and waiting for Tommy to reappear with his prisoner.

Naturally, other citizens in the area saw all the cops standing around and they stood around too and wondered what was going on. In minutes the word spread and still more people popped out of shops and came from around the corner and before long there were several hundred gawkers watching and craning their necks and talking sotto voce to one another as they awaited the next installment in Midvale's drama.

After about fifteen minutes the Chief was ready to send in a backup team when there was a stirring at the entrance to the hotel and a moment later Boyle came drifting out and struck a pose in the doorway for a second or two, then he adjusted his hat and started off down the street. He wore a sloppy, mile-wide grin and a vacant look in his eyes and a collective oohing sound rose from the crowd as he passed among them.

"Shit!" Hawes said.

"So much for the salami-like donniker theory," I said.

Eli came up then and said, "What the hell happened,

Chief?"

Hawes shrugged. "He got his brains fucked out, whatta you think happened?"

"You got a backup plan?" Eli demanded.

"Damn right," Hawes said. Then, to his men standing around gaping at the now brainless Tommy Boyle, he said, "Back inside, men! Come on, let's move it! Let's go!"

Everybody was herded back into the squad room and the Chief addressed them once more. "Men, the honor of the Midvale police department is at stake here. We've got one slip of a girl over there in that hotel and she's got the whole town buffaloed. Once this gets out we'll be the laughingstock of law enforcement everywhere, we'll never be able to go to a convention again and hold our heads up because we couldn't arrest one slip of a girl on a morals charge."

The men muttered among themselves and frowns and scowls appeared on their faces along with a determined look in every man's eye as each considered the gravity of their situation.

"I say we go over there and kick ass, by God!" Hawes cried. "I say we send a squad this time, four volunteers instead of one. And when she opens that door, we rush her ass and bam! slap the cuffs on her before she knows what the hell's goin' on."

A cheer broke from the ranks and every cop in the room stepped forward as one and the Chief smiled the satisfied smile of one whose hopes have just been realized. Four behemoths were chosen and they were dispatched to the hotel.

Once more everybody followed them outside and

across the street and another crowd gathered and this time we waited nearly half an hour before the four cops reappeared wearing the telltale grins and vacant looks of the fucked brainless.

People averted their eyes and ducked their heads and checked their watches as though suddenly remembering they had urgent business elsewhere and in no time the streets were devoid of spectators. Boyle and the four cops were rounded up and carted off to the hospital and the rest shook their heads and wandered off in twos and threes.

Chief Hawes, tightlipped and grim, said, "I'll get that bitch if it's the last thing I ever do!"

"Yeah, if you don't run out of cops first," I said.

He glared at me and strode off and I went back to the Beacon to start my Pulitzer Prize winning series of articles on Midvale's battle against the forces of evil.

CHAPTER TEN

Rev. Skaggs Falls And Plan C Is Hatched

The fat was in the proverbial fire now, of course. Word spread quickly about the fiasco on Friday and the succubus was the talk of the town. People stared fearfully up at the sixth-floor windows of the hotel and many crossed to the other side of the street when passing it. Young boys stood around in groups and bragged about how they'd like to see her try that stuff on them, by God, and their buddies concurred saying "Damn right!" and "You bet your ass!" and so on.

Young girls and women crossed themselves and sneered at the sixth-floor windows and cursed the men for not having the balls to drive the brazen hussy the hell out of town.

It was still a local matter, though, since there'd been no official pronouncement on the succubus. People relied on rumors and third-person accounts and outright lies for information and that was okay because most people would rather believe such sources than the facts, anyway.

On Saturday the Chief, Eli, Carl, and I met again at City Hall to devise a new scheme to rid the town of the succubus and save Midvale's male population from ruin.

"I say we hush it up," Eli said. "If word gets out we've got an oversexed demon living in Midvale, it could hurt business, make this a ghost town overnight."

Naturally, I was quick to resist this line of reasoning since there was no way I'd get my Pulitzer if I weren't allowed to write the story.

"Bullshit," I said. "The public has a right to know. What about the First Amendment? You can't censor the news, for Christ's sake, people'd never stand for it."

"By people you mean journalists," Carl said drily.

"By people I mean me," I said. "The Beacon'll run a series on the lady starting with Monday's edition. We're not about to sit on a story with national implications, period."

"Okay, but you'll turn Midvale into a circus," Eli said. "We'll have reporters and TV crews cluttering up every corner in town once word gets out we've got a beautiful woman here who fucks men brainless."

"We still haven't figured what to do about the succubus," the Chief said.

"Call in the health department," Eli said. "She's a health menace, isn't she? Let them worry about her."

"How's she a health menace?" Carl said. "Is she violating the pure food and drug laws or something?"

"Well, she's engagin' in unsafe sex," Eli said. "That's not healthy, is it?"

"Maybe not, but it's not a job for the health department," I said.

"What about the FBI?" Carl said. "Maybe she's violating our civil rights..."

"Or we could turn her over to Rev. Skaggs," Eli said. "You claim she's a demon and demons are church business, aren't they?"

"Hey, that's an idea," I said. "We send Skaggs in

after her to drive the demon out and if it works, great, our problem's solved. And if it doesn't work, we still win because she'll fuck his brains out for him."

"Humph," Eli said, "Skaggs hasn't got any brains now."

"I like it," Carl said.

"Me, too," the Chief said.

I stood up. "Good. It's him against the Devil. Tell him the whole town's counting on him, that we're all behind him."

"Yeah, way behind him," Carl said.

Eli reached for the phone and I headed back to the Beacon to continue my series on Midvale's mysterious Rolls-Royce woman while visions of Pulitzers danced in my head.

I knocked off at noon and met Ellen at Lola's for lunch as planned. She was looking especially nice in a skirt somewhat shorter than usual and a crisp blouse that contained what I was sure were braless boobs. Gad, but I'm fond of braless boobs.

"Yeah, she's a succubus, all right," I said. "I looked them up and she fits the description to a T."

"But they're only myths, old wives' tales," Ellen protested. "They only appear in dreams, they don't live in small town hotels and actually have intercourse with living people."

"This one does. I mean, I was there. Another minute and I'd a been a grinning sex maniac like those other poor saps."

"Yes, but you'd have had the ultimate fuck," she said, and there was a smile on her lips and a gleam in her eye that nearly equaled the one our succubus wore.

"Jesus, that's what it is, isn't it?" I said. "I never thought of it that way before."

"Does it make you feel like trying it yourself?" she said.

"Damn right it does," I said. "Come on." I took her hand and half pulled her from her seat.

"Wait a minute!" she said laughing. "I haven't finished my lunch."

"Forget lunch, we're going straight to dessert."

In six minutes flat we were in my apartment and the air was filled with flying blouses and shirts and underwear and a minute after that I gazed hungrily on her naked body. She smiled that sensual smile again and said mockingly, "Do I pass inspection?"

"Yeah," I said huskily. "C'mere."

And for the next thirty minutes I forgot all about succubi and demons and brainless fuckers and concentrated on the one immediately at hand.

And so the Midvale plot thickened and added a new and most welcome dimension for me.

Meanwhile, Eli had reached Skaggs and laid our proposition on him but the cagey old fraud bobbed and weaved and claimed he had a bad back and generally tried to nix the whole idea. But Eli pointed out how demons were church matters and what a boon it would be to his ministry if he succeeded in ridding our community of such a menace to the general health and morals of the populace and eventually convinced him it was worth the risk.

Skaggs himself spread the word that he would personally take on this foul creature and meet her face to face in a showdown that would pit the power of the Almighty against the forces of evil and the faithful were overjoyed. Hundreds appeared in front of Skaggs' house and the Reverend came out dressed in his preacher's robes and carrying an enormous Bible under one arm and a two-foot wooden cross in his hand. A mighty cheer went up and his aides passed amongst the crowd with their wicker baskets and the whole procession marched on the hotel in a grand display of faith and righteousness.

Once arrived, Skaggs harangued them again.

"There's an evil force in Midvale," he intoned, "an evil force that threatens all men, and God has directed me to do battle against this force and save the very soul of our Christian community from its evil. I hereby challenge this creature from the underworld, this vile and loathsome demon sent here by Satan to destroy Midvale, to a fight to the death, and with God's power I know I will be triumphant as no evil force can stand before the power of Almighty God!"

Ringing cries of support sounded on all sides. "Praise the Lord!" one shouted and another declaimed, "Show her no mercy!" and a third added "Strike her down, Rev. Skaggs!' and so on, and the ubiquitous wicker baskets surfaced again and were whisked through the crowd.

Skaggs scowled mightily and squared his shoulders, took up his cross and Bible, and bravely walked in to face the sexiest woman on Earth. A hush fell over the crowd as people leaned forward expectantly and stared up at the sixth-floor windows where they knew the battle would soon be joined. As for myself, I wanted a closer look this time and I followed Skaggs in and up to the sixth-floor and down the hall to her suite.

He banged on the door and it opened. Holding the cross before him, Skaggs stepped into the room and the door swung back but didn't quite shut. I sidled over and listened at the crack. I heard Skaggs say, "Come out, harlot! I hereby command that you be gone from our..."

He stopped in mid-sentence and I heard a thump as the Bible hit the floor. There was a heavy silence and then I heard Skaggs say, "Jesus Christ!" and I knew it wasn't a plea to the Almighty but rather an unconscious remark prompted by a his first vision of the world as a place filled with pudenda. A moment later there was the sound of heavy breathing and muttered oaths and thrashing about and falling furniture and assorted groans and moans and deep sighs.

It was all I could do to keep from widening the crack in the door to look in but I knew such a move would be fatal. If I laid eyes on her I'd be drawn in like iron filings to a magnet and she'd have two new brainless fuckees to add to her list of victims instead of just Skaggs.

When the commotion inside died down, I tiptoed away and sprinted off down the hall to the elevator and down to the lobby. I walked out on the sidewalk and the crowd surged forward in anticipation. "He's coming out," I said. "Stand back, give him some room."

A few moments later Skaggs came out of the hotel. He was dragging the Bible by some of its brightly colored ribbons and he held the cross listlessly in his other hand. Mainly, though, everybody gaped in wonder at the lopsided grin that adorned his mug. He swayed a bit on the steps and then started through the crowd in a kind of daze and the people fell back before him in shocked silence.

I saw Carl standing to one side and he came over to me. "What happened? I thought he was going to run her out of town?"

I shrugged and said, "I guess she didn't want to go."

Chief Hawes had a squad car standing by and Skaggs was bundled into it and hauled off to the hospital where he was given his very own copy of Playboy and fitted with boxing gloves so he wouldn't abuse himself. The crowd in front of the hotel watched him go with stunned looks on their faces and fear in their eyes for they'd just seen one of God's chosen overthrown by an evil force that would doubtless come after them next.

Everybody straggled off after a bit and Eli, Chief Hawes, and Carl followed me into Brady's where we split a pitcher of beer and analyzed the day's events.

"Okay, so we know we can't count on divine intervention," I said.

"At least we won't have to listen to that dope Skaggs anymore," Carl said.

"She should get the key to the city for that."

"But we're still stuck with a succubus," Eli said, "and if we don't do something pretty soon there won't be a man left in town with any brains in his head."

"So what's our next plan?" Carl said.

"I got it!" the Chief said. "We need a pro, the best

there is, a guy who's had a lot of experience dealin' with women and I know just the man." He paused for dramatic effect and then said, "Johnny Dicke!"

"The porn star?" Carl said.

"Hell, yes," Hawes said. "That guy's made over four hundred movies, they say he's fucked almost three thousand women, has a dick the size of a small log, and can go all night long."

"Maybe he's got something there," I agreed. "If endurance is a factor, Johnny's your man. I read he was shooting a movie in L.A. and he laid eight women in a single day and left that night on his honeymoon. The guy's a natural."

"Yeah, maybe he's just what the doctor ordered," Eli said. "I say we call him up and see what he says."

"How do we find him?" the Chief said.

"Easy," I said. "We just call the Actor's Guild. The guy has to have an agent and the agent'll know how to reach him. First, though, how much are we willing to pay for his services? This guy's a pro, he'll want money up front."

"Shit, pay him whatever the hell he wants," Eli snorted. "It'll be worth it to get her out of Midvale."

"Damn right," Chief Hawes said.

"Yeah, just get him here," Carl said.

So we came up with plan C and I launched a search for Johnny Dicke, the King of the Porno Flicks.

CHAPTER ELEVEN

Johnny Dicke Meets The Succubus

I decided to hold off on the story until after Johnny Dicke had a go at the Rolls-Royce woman on the grounds that it'd make an even better story if we solved our problem with a nationally known porn star. The tabloids would pay a fortune for a story like that, and so would a lot of other people.

Anyway, I called the Actor's Guild on Monday and got a phone number for Johnny's agent and gave him a ring. His name was Hennessey and he thought it was a crank call until I mentioned we were prepared to pay money.

I noticed an instant change in Hennessey's demeanor.

"You are, eh? Just how much did you have in mind?"

"How much would Johnny want?" I countered.

"All expenses and ten grand."

"Deal. How soon can he come?"

The canny devil grew suspicious then because it all sounded screwy even to a talent agent. "Hold on. How come you're willin' to pay ten grand just to get a lady laid?"

"Look, she's a fan of Johnny's, that's all," I said. "She's got more money than brains and she wants to get laid by a big star. It's an easy gig, a one-nighter,

Johnny won't even work up a sweat."

"Okay. Tomorrow. Where is this burg?"

I told him where Midvale was and agreed to arrange for tickets at LAX for that afternoon. I even booked them into the Midvale Manor so it'd be nice and convenient for them. That done, I batted out a story on the next tractor-pull contest at the fairgrounds for Saturday night and repaired to Lola's for lunch.

Lunch was delayed a bit, though, because I ran into Ellen on the way over and we decided to have another session of madcap lovemaking at my place first.

Once that was out of the way, I brought her up to date on the succubus.

"Johnny Dicke?" she said. "Ooh, he's handsome. I've seen some of his movies and he's, well, he's got a..."

She trailed off and I finished her thought for her. "Yeah, he's hung like a stallion. In fact, that's what we're counting on. If he can't straighten her out, nobody can."

"If he's anything like he is in his movies, I'd say she's in big trouble. The man's a machine, a lovemaking machine."

"He better be good because this lady's a real pro herself, you know. You saw what happened to those other guys. If Johnny's not as good as we think he is, he'll end up with a mile-wide smile and a fetish for pictures of naked girls."

"I say he can do it," she said. "Johnny Dicke won't let you down."

"If he does we just move on to plan D."

"What is plan D?"

"We don't know yet. Come on, let's go get some lunch. All this sex stuff makes me hungry."

She batted her eyes and gave me a coquettish look and reached for the currently unreachable. "What's your hurry? We haven't even had our dessert yet."

"Are you kidding? We've eaten every morsel in the larder and it won't be restocked any time soon, either."

"But I'm still hungry," she pouted.

"All I can offer you is dessert at Lola's," I said with a shrug.

She reluctantly agreed to settle for that but I could see she wasn't too happy about it.

Chief Hawes and I drove to the airport the next afternoon to pick Johnny up and I must admit I was impressed. He was a good-looking six-footer with curly blond hair and a ready smile and he wore tight-fitting pants with a substantial bulge hinting at the small log hidden therein. It was plain to see he'd be the kind of guy who'd have good luck with the ladies, and his being a sex flick stud made him all the more desirable.

In fact, he'd been recognized on the plane and a number of women were openly admiring him as he deplaned. Some even asked for his autograph and we had to wait a minute or two to say hello. His manager was a fat guy with a bushy moustache and pig-like eyes and looked like a guy who'd taken grad courses in wheeling and dealing. If there was an angle to be exploited, this guy'd find it.

Anyway, Johnny finally broke away from his admirers and the Chief and I introduced the boys.

"You said ten grand," Hennessey said. "Johnny always gets paid up front."

"I didn't bring the check with me," I said, "but he can have it as soon as we get back to Midvale."

"So who's this bimbo you want fucked?" Johnny said as we started for the car. "She must be some special number if she'll to pay ten grand just to get laid."

"Oh, she's unique, all right," I said. "This lady's so special you should be paying her for the privilege. A lot of guys who've had her claim she's the best lay in the whole world."

Johnny laughed and said, "Then we're even 'cause when she gets me she's getting the best stud in the whole world."

"Yeah, this oughta be somethin' to see," Hawes said drily. He looked askance at me and winked.

We got back to Midvale around six-thirty and checked our guests in before going to dinner at Luigi's, one of the better restaurants in town. It was a memorable meal. Everybody seemed to know Johnny on sight, especially the women. Our waitress was all smiles the whole time and fawned over Johnny like he was visiting royalty, and every woman in the place ogled him shamefully. I realized that they were inordinately familiar with him and that could only mean they must spend a helluva lot of their spare time watching his videos. What would their husbands think if they knew?

And Ellen was as bad as the worst of them. When she found out we were eating at Luigi's, she insisted she join us so she could meet Johnny personally.

She wore a dress that gaped immodestly every time

she leaned forward to retrieve the bread sticks or get more butter and she hung on Johnny's every word and generally made a spectacle of herself. Still, they were all equally guilty and Johnny reveled in it.

"How do you do it, Johnny?" I asked at one point. "How can you lay so many women and still keep going?"

"It's all in the genes," he said, "and you can spell it either way. My old man was a swinger, too. He laid every housewife within ten miles of our house. It's really kind of like an art, you know, not everybody can pull it off."

"I know," Ellen sighed, looking at me.

"So what's the story on this dame?" Hennessey asked. "She some kind of nymphomaniac or somethin'?"

"You could say that," I said warily. "She's sort of like Johnny, I guess. I mean, she's a pro, the best lay in the whole world according to every guy who's had her. In fact, most of them are so impressed with her they can hardly even talk about it afterwards."

Johnny grinned broadly and downed a glass of wine in a single swallow.

"She's like me, eh?" he said. "This oughta be some lady. When do I get to meet this bimbo?"

"Tonight, probably," I said. "You might want to ease up on the wine a bit."

He waved me off. "No problem. Drunk or sober, Johnny Dicke gets the job done."

"Yeah," Hennessey said, "it don't make any difference to Johnny. Drunk or not, a bimbo's a bimbo and he nails them all and nails them good."

"Yeah, you could say it's all in the wrist—except that's not where it is at all, man," Johnny said. "First, you need a first-rate dick, a dick like mine. Women like a big dick. Oh, I know, they all say it doesn't matter but it does. Ask them. If they tell the truth, they like them big. Right, girls?"

He turned and looked at Ellen and the waitress where they were watching with mouths open and vacant stares. They came to and smiled embarrassed smiles and made no comment.

And so it went. Johnny regaled us with stories of his wild experiences making porno movies and his endless exploits both on and off screen and in no time dinner was over and we started back to the hotel.

The Chief had already arranged to post cops all around the hotel and he had a squad car standing by to rush Johnny to the psycho ward if his famed donniker let him down. Since we'd told no one what Johnny was up to there were no crowds in the streets waiting to see the outcome of this titanic struggle between evil and evil, a fact for which we'd be grateful later.

We got back to the hotel and Johnny insisted on stopping in the bar for another drink. I toyed with a glass of orange juice while he put away a couple of quick vodka tonics and told ever more ribald tales of celluloid sex. I was getting nervous because I didn't want to send a helpless man into the Rolls-Royce woman's lair, but he assured us he could handle the booze and the odd floozie so I figured what the hell, he should know what he's doing.

"Where is this bimbo?" Johnny said after a while. "Is she in or isn't she?"

At that moment a guy standing at the bar looked out into the foyer at someone passing by and all of a sudden an enormous hard-on popped out of nowhere and thrust itself forward as though trying to reach its target from the bar.

"Yeah, I think she's in," I said. "You ready?"

"Don't worry, Johnny's always ready," Hennessey said. "He makes his livin' bein' ready. Right, Johnny?"

"Right," Johnny said. "Just let me go tap a kidney and we'll go fix the little lady up."

A few minutes later we were on our way to the sixth-floor. When we got off the elevator Joe Moran, the afternoon bookkeeper, was waiting to get on. The sloppy grin on his face and bright gleam in his eyes told the whole story. I was afraid Johnny would be alarmed if he discovered Joe looked like that because he'd just had his brains fucked out by the very lady he was en route to see so I took diversionary action.

I threw an arm around Joe's shoulders and said, "Joe, you old sonofagun, great makeup! Perfect. That look'll bowl them over. You've got it down just right."

As I talked I steered him onto the elevator and hit the down button as he stood facing the rear wall. Johnny and Hennessey looked back at Joe with puzzled expressions. They turned to me as the doors closed on the hapless Joe.

"What's with him?" Johnny demanded. "The guy looks like the town idiot, for Christ's sake."

"No, no," I said, "that's Joe Moran. He's trying out for a part in a play called, uh, 'The Idiots.' He's just rehearsing his part, that's all."

"Well, he's a goddam natural," Hennessey said.

"The guy looks totally brainless."

"Her suite's this way," I said, moving along the hall toward room 666.

"Is this bimbo expecting me?" Johnny asked.

"Uh, not formally, but I'm pretty sure she's ready for you," I said. We reached 666 and stopped. "This is it. Uh, Mr. Hennessey, if you'd like to go back down and wait with the Chief, we'll get things underway here."

"Yeah, come on, Mr. Hennessey," the Chief said, "I'll buy you a good cigar."

"Ten minutes, Johnny," Hennessey said. "I'll be in the bar."

"You got it," Johnny said.

They started back down the hall and I turned to Johnny. "You ready, Johnny?"

"The question is, man, is she ready?"

I punched the doorbell and took two or three steps down the hall and away from any possible fallout from stray pheromones. The door opened and Johnny looked at me, grinned, and stepped into the room. I turned and raced to 664 and ducked inside. I crossed the room in a single leap and climbed out through the window and onto the fire escape that ran past her windows. We'd hidden a video camera outside her window earlier and it was aimed straight into the room. I wanted to make sure it was in position and running.

Naturally, I didn't look in the window or I'd have run the risk of being mesmerized and turned idiotic myself, but the camera ground away faithfully and spared me such a fate. The window was closed so I wasn't able to hear anything, but my imagination ran amuck and I conjured up visions of Johnny nailing her evil ass to the floor with his log-sized donniker as she writhed in joyous agony, soared to a dozen exploding climaxes in a row, and was utterly destroyed by the terrible wonder of Johnny's massive member.

Alas, it didn't turn out that way. After about half an hour there was a shout from the street below and Johnny reeled from the hotel and out onto the sidewalk wearing the usual slaphappy smile and holding his battered and scarred and now dishrag-limp, log-sized dick in his hand. Some women nearby gasped and fainted dead away at the sight and strong men blanched and turned away. Hennessey was aghast and clutched his throat and staggered back a step or two.

"My God!" he cried. "What the hell happened?!"

"Nothin' much," Chief Hawes said. "He just got his brains fucked out, that's all."

So they packed Johnny into the squad car and took off for Dr. Bane's booby hatch. Hennessey went along and moaned the whole time about how poor Johnny would never work again and we'd be hearing from his lawyer and so on.

I took the camera and went down to join Chief Hawes and Eli where they stood gazing absently at the receding squad car.

"There goes plan C," I said wistfully.

"Yeah," Eli said.

The Chief sighed. "The poor bastard never had a chance," he said.

"Let's go have a look at the tape," I said. "Maybe we can see how the hell she does it."

We headed back to the station to view what was

probably the last X-rated video Johnny Dicke would ever make.

CHAPTER TWELVE

Plan C-1—The Phony Donniker Ploy

Eli, Carl, the Chief, and I assembled in the Chief's office and Off. Meikowski plugged the camera into the TV. Meikowski was a young rookie cop about twenty-two or so who'd only been on the force a few months. She was pert and chipper and pretty, but very professional and businesslike. Anyway, when she was all set up, she looked at the Chief and said, "Ready, Chief."

He looked at the rest of us. "You guys all set?"

"I don't know," Eli said uncertainly. "What if...?"

He trailed off and Carl said, "Yeah, what if she hexes us again? Maybe seeing her on tape'll be just as bad as seeing her in person."

"Hey, it's a tape," I said. "We've all seen X-rated tapes before, it's like seeing a movie, that's all. Besides, the pheromones can't get at us from a tape. We've got nothing to worry about here."

"Shit, Grogan's right," the Chief said. "Roll them, Meikowski."

"Yessir."

She pushed the tape in, fiddled with some buttons, and there was Johnny on the screen with an enormous hard-on that whipped and thrashed around like it was filled with coiled springs and suddenly I felt somebody's hands gripping my shoulders. I turned and got a glimpse of Meikowski standing behind me and she was wearing a look commonly worn by women in the middle of a first-class orgasm.

Before I could deal with that, I saw the succubus pop into view and I forgot all about Meikowski. I'd been wrong, of course. She no sooner appeared than we were all spellbound again and gaped like voyeurs ogling topless bathers on a Riviera beach. She moved with wonderful grace and symmetry and sensuality, her gaze fixed on poor Johnny whose dork jumped and jerked spasmodically in anticipation. She slowly, tantalizingly, took off the thin gown she was wearing and advanced on Johnny.

Johnny was already ruined, of course. His eyes bulged and he licked dry lips and stared straight at her pulsing pudendum. The two of them came together in mid-room and in a split second were locked in a tangled embrace and fell to the floor in what seemed like slow motion. Meikowski dug her nails into my shoulders and thrust herself into my back and made little squealing noises in my ear, but I was too busy with my own searing libido to pay much attention to her and hers.

We sat transfixed, defenseless, vulnerable, enormous hard-ons pulsating drum-like as we watched Johnny fucked brainless by the greatest lay in the whole world. Then it was over. She rose and stood naked over Johnny, her boobs heaving and a smile on her face that was at once a look of satisfaction and exuberance, pleasure and triumph. Johnny sat up and the sloppy grin was already plastered on his face.

He stood and took two or three rocky steps before

gaining control of his limbs and left. She closed the door behind him and then turned and looked straight at the camera and smiled a smile that seemed to challenge us to come up with a better scheme next time. A moment later she moved from the camera's view and the room went dark as she turned out the lights.

The tape ran through the camera silently as we stared at it for a long minute or so, then we looked at each other and five minds clicked as one.

Meikowski, aroused well beyond the point of no return, reached up and ripped her shirt open and sent buttons flying in all directions as she unloosed two exquisite, melon-like boobs with jaunty nipples standing like little sentinels and we unzipped our pants and whipped out our donnikers and headed in her direction.

Fortunately for all of us, Wally Hicks came in then with a req for Chief Hawes to sign and he saw what was going on. He reached us just as we reached Meikowski and the six of us fell together in a wild tangle of tits and legs and hard-ons and crashed into furniture and made a lot of noise that brought other cops to see what the hell was going on. Somebody dragged in a garden house and poured a stream of cold water on all of us and we finally cooled down enough to fall back and gasp for breath.

Wally thoughtfully helped Meikowski put her boobs back in her shirt and he was considerate enough to use only his elbows. The rest of us stuffed somewhat deflated dorks back into our pants and tried to assume an indifferent look.

"Okay, Wally, that'll be all," the Chief said.

"Uh, yeah, uh, sure, Chief," Wally said. He looked at the others and they shrugged and retreated with their hose and curiosity. Once they'd gone, we looked at each other.

"Jesus Christ," Carl said.

"Yeah," Eli concurred.

"That's got to be the greatest fuck movie of all time!" Chief Hawes said.

"Hey, what's with you, Meikowski?" I said. "She isn't supposed to turn you on."

"Who said I was watching her?" she demanded. "She wasn't the only one getting laid on that tape, you know."

"Okay, okay," the Chief said, "so now we've seen the tape. So let's get back to work around here."

Meikowski held her shirt together to keep her boobs from leaking out again and stared at Hawes with a look that even Ray Charles would have recognized. "I'm taking the rest of the day off, Chief," she said quietly. "I have to get...I have something to do."

"Yeah, sure, Meikowski," he said. "You go ahead."

"Right," Eli said. "You earned it."

Meikowski left and we watched her go. After a moment, I said, "Jesus, we can't even watch the woman on tape."

"So," Hawes said, "what's plan D?"

"Ask her what the hell she wants and give it to her before she fucks everybody's brains out," Eli said.

"You mean give up?" Carl said. "You want us to turn Midvale over to a spiritual sexpot? Why, Nathan Hale would be outraged, George Washington would turn over in his grave at any such thought."

"Oh, yeah?" Eli said. "They wouldn't think anything if they ran into this babe. They wouldn't have any brains to think with."

"Eli's right," Hawes said. "She's too much for us. Johnny was the best we had; we don't have any backups."

"Wait a minute here," I said. "There's got to be something we can do. We owe it to Midvale, to the good citizens of this town who look to us for leadership and protection. We can't let this glorified hooker take over our town without putting up a fight. I say we give it one more try, let's put our heads together and come up with a plan that'll work this time."

"I'm with Grogan," Carl said. "What the hell have we got to lose? If we fight and lose, so what? We're all goners anyway."

"But maybe this is a bigger problem than we think," the Chief said. "I mean, what if we're in over our heads here? This lady may turn out to be a threat to the entire planet and we should be bringin' in the National Guard or maybe even the Marines."

"But then the whole world would know we got us a succubus," Eli protested. "We'd be on the national news by tomorrow night and..."

"And we'd all be rich," I said. "Look, Eli, you're afraid publicity would turn Midvale into a circus, that's what you said the other day. But think for a minute. Would that hurt us? I mean, people would come from all over the globe to get a look at a real succubus. They'd fill up our hotels and buy our souvenirs and eat in our restaurants and..."

"Hey, how about a contest!" Carl cried. "We could

offer a million dollar prize to any man who could lay the succubus and beat her at her own game!"

"Yeah, every macho guy out there would want a crack at her," Hawes said.

"Midvale would be the hottest spot on the map..." I said.

"And everybody in town would make a fortune!" Eli cried. "You're right, Grogan, a succubus could make this town!"

"I bet there's even a movie deal in it," the Chief said. "We could sell the rights to Paramount and shoot the thing right here in town!"

"We might even get parts in the movie," Carl said. "Maybe we could be extras."

"Then it's agreed," I said. "I break the story in the Beacon and we put in a call for help. Chief, maybe you could call in the feds. Eli, you cable the governor and ask for the National Guard, but not before my story is out. Agreed?"

All nodded and plan D went into action.

Actually, as it turned out, there was an interim plan I might call plan C-1 that unexpectedly popped up on Wednesday, but in terms of our formal planning it wasn't our idea so maybe it shouldn't count.

On Wednesday I reported to the Beacon early, that is, early for me. I got there about ten a.m. and worked on the first installment of the succubus story and it was heavy going. Just writing about her brought erotic images that clouded my mind, raised my blood pressure and donniker, and produced a lot of literary lapses that did serious harm to my usually brilliant prose.

I kept at it, though, and made good progress until almost lunchtime when Art came hurrying in and said, "She got them all, Grogan, every damn one of them!"

"Who got who?"

"The succubus. She got the auditors, all eight of them. They're here to audit the bank, they just checked in at the hotel last night and today they're all hanging around the lobby grinning like crazy and lifting up ladies' skirts and acting like they're nuts or something."

"Holy shit!" I said. "Are they still there? In the hotel?"

"Yeah. I just came from there."

"Okay, look, get Chief Hawes. Tell him to get some cars over there, but not squad cars. Maybe we can get them out of town before everybody finds out what happened."

Art nodded and started out and I followed him. On the way over I raced down to Kaz's drugstore and grabbed a handful of Playboys and Penthouses and sped back to the hotel. I entered the lobby and all eight of them were grinning like hyenas and leering at any females who happened by. I held up a centerfold and waved it for all to see.

"Who wants a Playboy?" I sang out. "Just came in, pictures of naked cheerleaders. Get them while they're hot."

The auditors fixed on that centerfold like baby ducks imprinting on the nearest moving object and I led them in a bunch to a corner of the lobby where they'd be easier to collect when Hawes showed up. I handed out magazines and they were instantly absorbed in naked girls and carnal thoughts. A few minutes later the Chief huffed in with some cops and they hustled the auditors out and into unmarked cars and whisked them away to Dr. Bane's nut ward.

Chief Hawes and I stood on the sidewalk and watched them go. "Jesus Christ, Grogan, she got eight at once that time!"

"Yeah, we're in deep shit here, Chief. If she starts knocking them off eight at a time, none of us'll have any brains by Christmas."

"I say we call in the feds right now," he said firmly.

I could see my scoop vanishing before my eyes. "Wait one more day," I said. "My story comes out tomorrow and it'll be on the wire services by the afternoon. We can call them then. What's one more day?"

"Are you kiddin'? This broad could wipe out a regiment in twenty-four hours."

"Maybe she's pooped after last night. Give me another day. In twenty-four hours the whole world'll know and you can flood the town with feds and Marines and the Foreign Legion."

"Okay, you win, Grogan, but tomorrow's the deadline. If this broad's gonna wipe out the planet, I don't want to be the guy who gets blamed for it."

"Tomorrow it is, not a minute later. Thanks, Chief."

"Humph," he said.

Chief Hawes went out to the hospital to check on the latest victims and I wandered over to Ellen's office and met her on her way out.

"You hear about the auditors?" I asked.

"What auditors?"

"Then you haven't heard. The Rolls-Royce woman got eight of them last night. They haven't got a whole brain among them now."

"Eight? She got eight auditors at one time?"

I nodded. "Caught them in one of the conference rooms. Poor devils are mostly wimpy guys, you know, the kind of guys who can't handle regular women let alone supernatural ones."

"And you can handle regular women?" she said with a trace of a smile.

"Sure. Let's go to my place and I'll prove it."

She hesitated and bit a lip and I knew she was thinking it over. Then she said, "I really can't now. I've got an appointment in twenty minutes and..."

I leaned close and said, "Twenty minutes is a long time."

She made up her mind and quickly unlocked her office and we went inside. She locked the door behind us and hurried into her inner office and turned to face me. Her face was suddenly flushed and she reached down and slid her skirt over her hips and ten minutes later a badly disheveled Ellen lay with an errant boob leaking out of her blouse and panting heavily. She puffed at a stray lock of hair and grinned at me and said, "Okay, so you can handle regular women."

I grinned back at her and we assembled ourselves and left, she for her appointment and me for Lola's. I ran into Ezra Halley there and he took me aside and whispered some nonsense about aliens before heading to Zak's drugstore for the latest space mags.

I had the diet special, a quarter-pound 'burger with

onion rings and fries and a slice of lemon meringue pie with low cal meringue. After lunch I sauntered out and stood on the sidewalk while unwrapping a slim Macanudo and surveyed Main Street. I'd just lit up when an old codger ambled up and spoke to me.

"Heard about those auditor fellas," he said.

"Hmm?" I said.

"Over at the hotel. The Rolls-Royce woman got them. You was there, you saw them."

"Oh, yeah, those auditors. What about them?"

"I know how to stop her, that's what."

"You do? How?"

"With this," he said, and he stuck a hand into his pocket and proceeded to produce a mighty dork which leapt upward and outward in a series of violent thrusts against the restraining cloth of his trousers. In no time he had a hard-on that would have compared favorably to Johnny Dicke's and I was duly impressed.

"That's pretty impressive," I said, "but so what? A guy your age can't go up against the Rolls-Royce woman. She'd chew your ass up and never work up a sweat."

"Oh, yeah?" he rejoined. "For your information, Mr. Wise Guy, I got a secret weapon. That ain't my real dick in there. I got me one of those implants, a phony dick I pump up an' it stays up until I hit the release button. I figure she can fuck all day an' I'll still be stiff as a board."

Now I was impressed. "No shit?" I said. "Maybe you've got something there. Nobody's tried a phony dick before. Maybe she'd be so frustrated she'd give up and hit the road if she found one she couldn't turn into the consistency of cooked spaghetti."

He thwacked it a good shot to demonstrate its resiliency and said, "Don't worry, pal, that ain't gonna happen."

Shit, what could we lose? He was a volunteer, wasn't he? Who's to say a man shouldn't be allowed to volunteer for a dangerous mission just because he's an old-timer? Should brave, patriotic deeds be limited to the fit and able?

Certainly not.

"What's your name, friend?" I said.

"Name's Roy," he said. "And you're Grogan, right?"

"Right. Come on, Roy. Let's give it a try."

We went to the police station and ran into Chief Hawes on the way. He'd just come back from the hospital and he was looking for me.

"Hey, Grogan, I just talked to Doc Bane. He says..." He noticed Roy then. "Who's this?"

"This is Roy, Chief," I said. "Roy's a civic-minded citizen who's got an idea about how to fix our lady friend. Tell him, Roy."

"I got a phony dick, Chief. See?" And he reeled the thing out right there on Main Street and held it in both hands while it lunged and spat angrily as though it had a mind of its own. A woman nearby gazed in awe-struck wonder at Roy's dick and the Chief was so surprised he jumped back and threw an arm up in a defensive position.

"Hey, for Christ's sake, put that thing away!" he cried. "You can't go around with your dick out on Main Street!"

Roy dutifully reeled it back in and I said, "It's not a real dick, Chief. It's one of those penile implants they've got now. You pump them up with a little pump they sew inside your groin. Things are like iron, Roy says it won't go down until he hits the release valve."

"So Roy's got a fake dick, so what?" Hawes said. "He still can't wave the thing all over Main Street."

"But don't you get it, Chief? Roy says he can knock off the succubus with it. She won't be able to make it go down if she fucks him all night long."

"What? You'd send an old guy like this up against the greatest lay in the hole world? Are you crazy? Look what she did to Johnny. How's an old coot like this gonna...?"

"But Johnny has a real dick. Roy's is like a garden hose, it's practically fuck proof. I say he's got a shot, a real shot."

The Chief looked at Roy and frowned. "Is that right?" he said. "You really think you can knock this lady off?"

"You damn tootin,'" Roy said. "I'll fuck her brains out, you see if I don't."

The Chief looked at me and shrugged.

"Then we do it?" I said.

"Okay, but have Carl draw up a statement that the town's not responsible if anything goes wrong. I don't want to end up bein' sued."

"That okay with you, Roy?" I said.

"Sure, I'll sign anything," he said. "What the hell, I'm seventy-eight years old, what can happen to a guy seventy-eight that ain't already happened to him?"

"Spoken like a real trouper, Roy," I said. "Come on,

let's see Carl and get that statement."

We found Carl in the City Hall and laid the proposition on him.

"So that's it, Carl," I said. "How's it look? Legally, I mean."

"Well, if it's strictly voluntary and done of his own free will, I guess it'll work. I'll just make up a disclaimer and if Roy signs it, why, go ahead."

And that's what we did. Roy put his John Hancock on the dotted line and Chief Hawes, Carl, and I took him across the street to the hotel. The Chief alerted a squad car to stand by out front and Doc Gramble came over and hung out in the lobby in case Roy suffered some trauma and needed first-aid.

Once the stage was set, the Chief and Carl took Roy upstairs while I waited in the lobby with Doc. I'd been feeling a little, well, horny lately; I mean, hornier than usual since I'd always had an eye for a well-turned ankle and seldom went fifteen minutes without an erotic thought, but here lately I'd been walking around with half a hard-on most of the time. I thought maybe I'd been around the succubus too much and some of the fallout pheromones had seeped into my system so I wanted to minimize the risk.

Anyway, Doc and I talked about the succubus while we waited.

"I saw Bill Swigert yesterday and he looked pretty good, Doc," I said. "In fact, he looked almost like his old self."

"He just about is," Doc said. "The slaphappy grin's gone down a good bit and he talks pretty much like he always did, but he's still got a pussy fetish."

"Well, if that's all, he's back to normal then. What guy doesn't have a pussy fetish?"

"True enough, but it's something more than a normal interest in sex. For instance, he's always ogling pictures of naked women and walks around with two-thirds of a hard-on and even propositions women."

"Hell, we all..."

"No, it's more than that. It's like there's been some kind of mental change, or even a personality change, that's centered around sex and women and centerfolds and eroticism generally. Remember, Bill, and this Wahl guy, too, neither of them were what you'd call ladies' men before they ran into our succubus, but since then they think of nothing else."

"But they still function like normal people? I mean, in other ways?"

"Seem to. But the point is, it's changed them in some basic way. Who knows, maybe in time it will all wear off, but it's like they were infected with a virus and there's still traces of it in them."

We fell silent for a moment and watched a gorgeous creature cross the lobby in a red silk dress that looked painted on. She boarded the elevator and when the door closed behind her we both sighed audibly and stared vacantly into the middle distance while our libidos did wonderful tricks in our minds' eye.

After nearly an hour had passed we began pacing restlessly and eyeing the clock and frowning. Could something have gone wrong? Even Johnny hadn't lasted a whole hour.

"We better go take a look," Doc said at last. "Maybe she came out and nailed Carl and Chief Hawes, too."

"Good idea," I said. We started for the elevator when the door opened and Carl stepped out. He wore a worried look.

"What's going on, Carl?" I said. "Roy's been up there almost an hour and..."

"Roy's dead," he said.

"Dead?"

"Are you sure?"

"You can't tell from looking at him, but he's deader than a mackerel, all right. I got to go get a stretcher."

He disappeared outside and Doc and I hopped into the elevator and sped to the sixth-floor. Once arrived, we hurried down the hall to 666 and found Chief Hawes in the hall standing over a motionless form covered with a blanket and we saw why Carl had equivocated over the appearance of death. Roy was lying on his back and an enormous hard-on rose up magisterially and lifted the blanket high into the air like the center pole on a tent. Doc pulled the blanket back to check him out and Roy was grinning from ear to ear and was altogether the happiest of corpses.

"He died laughin,'" the Chief said somberly. "He was in there almost an hour and he was yellin' like a cowboy on a buckin' bronco and raisin' Cain and then it got real quiet and a minute later he came out laughin' and grinnin' and he just keeled over and died on the spot."

"His heart gave out," Doc said. "His phony dick worked fine but his heart couldn't take the strain."

"Looks like he died a happy man, though," I said.

"Why not?" Doc said. "He just had the greatest lay in the whole world. Any man could die with a smile on his face after that."

Carl and two cops came down the hall then carrying a stretcher and they loaded Roy on it and started off toward the elevator. Doc took his hat off and hung it on Roy's tent-pole dick in an effort to disguise it somewhat as they carried him through the lobby but people still stared open-mouthed at the sight as we passed them.

Since he was already a goner, the cops carried Roy down the street and straight to Gilroy's funeral parlor. Gilroy studied the corpse for a minute and said, "How the hell am I gonna get this guy in a casket? We'll have to drill a hole in the lid for his dick to stick through."

"Maybe you can lash it down with baling wire," the Chief said.

"Or bury him face down and drill the hole through the bottom so it won't show," Carl said.

"Or cut it off," I said. "Hell, he won't need it where he's gone."

"But it's against the law to mutilate a corpse," Gilroy said. "You want me to lose my license?"

"You figure it out," the Chief said. "We only make deliveries. Send the bill to City Hall."

We marched out and went to Brady's where we ordered pitchers of beer and lit up stogies and reflected on the vicissitudes of dealing with supernatural phenomena in the natural world and we stayed there for the rest of the afternoon.

CHAPTER THIRTEEN

The Midvale Succubus Goes National

That night I had dinner with Ellen at Luigi's and we drank a bottle of red wine with our linguine and then repaired to the bar where she drank something with little umbrellas in it and I worked over a couple of Scotches and we talked about the topic that had come to be an obsession in Midvale.

After a while the mayor came in and joined us at the bar. "I heard about Roy," he said. "Too bad. He did pretty good for an old-timer, didn't he?"

"Sure, but don't forget he had a bionic dick," I said. "He wouldn't have lasted two minutes if he used his real one."

"Say," Ellen said, "maybe that's the answer. You need some kind of mechanical penis, maybe a rubber one or plastic or something, one that stays hard no matter what."

"A dildo!" I said. "If we could get her to fuck one of those big rubber dildos she'd end up fucking her own brains out."

"They even come with electric motors," Ellen said excitedly. "You can get ribbed ones and ones with big warts all over them and in different colors and sizes..." Suddenly she stopped in mid-sentence and blushed prettily. "At least, that's what I read somewhere," she added lamely.

"But how would we get her to go for a dildo if we got one?" I said. "She seems pretty familiar with real dorks now; I don't think you'd be able to fool her with a rubber one."

"Good point," Eli said.

"Wait a minute, we already tried that anyway," I said. "When she made it with Roy she was actually on a phony one, wasn't she? Wouldn't that be the same as a dildo?"

"No, because dildos don't have hearts," Ellen said. "From what you said, Roy gave her a run for her money until his heart gave out. If he didn't have a heart, she'd still be straddling Roy's indestructible penis and getting nowhere."

"Okay, so it might work," I said, "but we still don't know how to pull it off. And after tomorrow we won't be the ones making the decisions around here. Once the feds take over nobody will give a damn what any of us think."

"You're right," Ellen said glumly. Then, brightly, "But it'll be good for business."

And good for Pulitzer Prizes, too, I thought. After more small talk Eli wandered off and Ellen and I went back to my place and I played the Johnny Dicke tape for her. Half an hour later a delegation from the pool hall arrived at our door and demanded we cut out the racket or else, by God.

On Thursday I ran into Ezra again and he said he hadn't seen a single alien in days but he was keeping his eyes open. Reassured, I ordered Lola's pancakes in real maple syrup with pork sausages and scrambled eggs on the side and saved some calories by skipping sugar in my coffee. One has to be health conscious, you know.

I lit up a cigar after breakfast and drew howls of protest from somebody in the back who raved on about air pollution or cancer or some such crap but I ignored them. It's amazing how many half-wits there are who'll never be satisfied till they take every last bit of pleasure out of life and replace it with dreariness. Somebody ought to tell them nobody gets out of this life alive anyway, so they may as well relax and enjoy it while they can.

I went to the Beacon and made a few small changes in my breaking succubus story before Tom and Art started the presses for Thursday's edition. I was composing Pulitzer Prize acceptance speeches in my head when Bert came in.

"That's a mighty big story, Grogan," he said. "It's going to turn the state upside down, maybe even Washington. You're real sure about your facts, I take it?"

"Chief Hawes and Eli can verify every one of them. She's a bona fide succubus, all right, and she's all ours. Midvale'll be the talk of the whole country once this story hits the wires." He still seemed dubious so I added, "Why? You got some reservations?"

"Nope, but most people don't think there's any such thing as a real succubus. They aren't gonna believe she is one."

"But if she isn't a succubus, what the hell is she?" I said defensively.

"I don't know. Could be anything. I'm just sayin' they're gonna think we're crazy, that's all. It's almost like sayin' we've got a real ghost stayin' over at the hotel."

"Whatever she is, nobody's seen anything like her before. Succubus or ghost or figment of our imagination, somebody's got to do something about her before every guy in town is sans brains and addicted to dirty magazines."

"Okay, we just report the news," Bert said. "A story's a story, we'll let the experts figure it out."

And we did. The paper came out at two o'clock as usual and Amos had them on the street fifteen minutes later. The entire edition sold out in two hours and Bert ran a second edition that night for distribution the next morning. It seems half the population of Midvale was on the streets in groups large and small as they discussed the ominous creature holed up in the hotel on Main Street.

The story was damn good journalism. We had pictures of the succubus that were taken when she was abroad in the town and she photographed so well I felt my hands get clammy as I looked at them. And the writing was as good as any I'd ever done.

I recounted her arrival and her effect on our citizenry and our first attempts to approach her. I included quotes from credible citizens on their reactions to the succubus and statements from Drs. Gramble and Bane on the condition of her victims. And, finally, I explained how I'd learned she was a succubus and gave an account of how such creatures prey on innocent men and turn them into a kind of sexual zombie.

In short, the story had everything, mystery and sex and intrigue and ominous hints of potential violence.

It invoked the spirit world and magic and evil forces and mysticism and fear. And it ended on a note of desperation with the town's appeal for help from the governor and feds because the succubus had thwarted our best efforts to get her out of Midvale and save the people from her cruel assault.

Eli called the governor's office in the capital and reported our succubus as planned and Chief Hawes alerted the FBI in the city. The governor flat out didn't believe it and sent an aide down to check up on the mayor and see if he'd lost his marbles altogether.

I was there when the Chief called the FBI and they were pissed at him for taking up their valuable time with cock and bull stories.

"Look," the Chief said, "we got a goddam succubus who's fuckin' everybody's brains out down here and I'm makin' an official report to you people. I suggest you get somebody down here and do it quick. What? Yeah, that's what I said. We've got a dozen guys walkin' around town without a brain in their heads and we know she's the one who's responsible. Suit yourself, but the story's already gone out and the whole country'll know by this time tomorrow. You'll have Congress on your ass if you don't get somebody down here." He hung up and scowled. "The assholes think I'm drunk or crazy."

"Are they sending somebody?"

"Yeah, but he wasn't happy about it. He said he'll send a couple of agents in the morning."

"Okay, so it's out of our hands now," I said. "We've done our duty, if the succubus reduces the entire town to imbecility it isn't our fault."

The Chief sighed and said, "So why do I feel this isn't over yet?"

Maybe because it isn't, I thought. And it wasn't. That night guests started leaving the hotel in droves when they found out they were living with a creature from the spirit world and the management slashed rates in an effort to keep at least some business. As it happened, a troop of Japanese professors who had come to study a typical dying small town in America showed up and headed for the Midvale Manor. They had some difficulty with English and couldn't quite follow the stories about succubi and brainless fuckees so they jumped at the low rates and moved in.

Needless to say, by breakfast the next day the succubus had laid every one of them and they were completely bereft of brains. The desk clerk notified Chief Hawes and he rounded all twelve of them up and whisked them out to Dr. Bane, but people saw them being loaded into some squad cars and the word spread all over town like wildfire. When the two FBI agents rolled into town about eleven o'clock there was an angry mob in front of the hotel demanding the succubus be arrested and bound over for trial on the charge of fucking people's brains out.

The feds went to the station to talk to Chief Hawes and Amos spotted them going in and tipped me off. I hurried over and got in on the briefing.

"You don't really expect us to believe she's a real succubus," Agent Skinner said.

"The hell I don't," the Chief said. "You think I'm makin' this crap up? You think we're small town hicks who don't know a succubus when we see one?"

"We're not saying that," Agent Brown said. "It's just that this is the twenty-first century and succubi belong in the Middle Ages. People just don't believe in spirits nowadays and we'd look pretty silly if we turned in a report that there was a succubus living in Midvale."

The Chief was pissed. "Okay, go find out for yourselves," he said. "Ring her bell and see what happens. She's in 666. But I'm tellin' you you're gonna come out with an IQ of fifty."

"Come on, George," Agent Skinner said, "Let's go take a look."

"Don't do it!" I cried. "The Chief's right, she's a bona fide succubus and she's already de-brained twenty-five guys. Stop by the hospital and check with Dr. Bane if you don't believe us. He runs the booby hatch out there and he'll let you talk to some of the victims."

Agent Brown shrugged. "What the hell, it won't hurt to see the doctor first."

So it was agreed and we started for the hospital. On the steps outside we ran into Eli who was with a fat guy carrying a briefcase and a foot-long cigar. Eli stopped us.

"Chief, this guy's from the governor's office," Eli said. "He's here about the succubus."

Chief Hawes extended his hand. "Pleased to meet.." he started to say but the fat guy interrupted him.

"What's all this crap about a succubus?" he demanded. "We got no time for this crap, we can't be chasing all over the state just because you guys can't arrest one lone, helpless woman, for God's sake."

"Okay, if it's so simple, you go arrest her," the Chief

said.

"By God, I will!" the fat guy said. "Where is this broad? If I throw her ass in the slammer, maybe you guys can take it from there and leave the governor the hell out of it."

"Room 666," the Chief said. "Hotel's right across the street."

Before anyone could stop him, the fat guy jammed his cigar in his mouth and strode off toward the hotel. We followed and gathered in the hotel bar to await results. Fifteen minutes later the fat guy sailed out of the elevator and across the lobby with the telltale grin on his mug and the vacant stare in his eyes that marked the brainless. Agents Skinner and Brown stared incredulously at the sight.

"Jesus Christ!" Agent Skinner said.

"Holy shit!" his partner said.

"Maybe now you'll believe us," Chief Hawes said. He signaled and a couple of cops grabbed the fat guy and tossed him in the squad car for the trip to the hospital.

"What happened to him?" Skinner demanded.

"Gentlemen, you've seen a man who's just enjoyed the greatest piece of ass on Earth—and paid for it with his brains," I said. "Now, are you going to help us get rid of the lady before we're all turned into morons?"

Agent Skinner turned to Brown. "Call headquarters. Tell them it's Code Red. We need a special squad down here and we need them fast. We'll stake the place out till they get here."

"Right," Brown said as he turned away cell phone in hand.

"Okay, Chief," Skinner said, "I'm taking over. I want the hotel surrounded twenty-four hours a day. If she tries to leave, I want her followed. And keep everybody away from her so we won't incur new casualties."

"Now you're talkin,'" the Chief said.

And so the federal government had arrived on the scene and would soon have everything under control—or so we thought.

CHAPTER FOURTEEN

Plan D Fails; Tension Mounts

Chief Hawes stationed a ring of cops around the hotel and people were kept away from the building so they wouldn't be contaminated by loose pheromones in the area or accidentally run into the succubus and be overcome right there in the middle of Main Street. All guests were ordered from the building, as were the staff people. The Midvale Manor, the town's stateliest caravansary, finally housed but a single guest, and an uninvited one at that.

People stood on the sidewalk in groups and frowned and gestured and looked apprehensively at the sixth-floor windows where "she" lived. The men watched with a peculiar look in their eyes that measured something half way between fear and lust, anxiety and longing. Being men, they were drawn inexorably by her unique sexuality as much or more than they were repelled by apprehension.

The women openly hated her more every day and became increasingly vocal about the failure of the town's men to get rid of her. There was even some talk of them taking things into their own hands and throwing the sexpot's ass the hell out of town themselves.

Later that afternoon I was leaving Chief Hawes' office when I saw a cop leading Horace Wahl toward the cellblock. Horace was wearing handcuffs and grinning to beat the band.

"Hey," I said, "what's he done? How come he's under arrest?"

"Don't ask me," the cop said. "I just lock them up."

I hurried back to the Chief's office and went in without knocking. "Chief, they've arrested Wahl! What the hell's going on?"

"I just got the report," he said. "Peeping Tom. Caught him out at the high school. He was up a tree with a pair of binoculars watchin' the girls' softball team takin' showers."

"You're kidding!" I said.

"Nope, caught him red-handed."

"But the guy was a church deacon. Why is he all of a sudden peeping at naked girls?"

"That's not all. Bill Swigert's wife filed for a divorce this mornin.' Seems she caught him layin' the Widow Barnes in the potting room. They were naked as jay birds and all covered with loam."

"What?! Swigert, too? It's that goddam succubus. She's turned the poor bastards into satyrs. They'll never have a rational thought again."

"It sure looks that way. If she keeps layin' guys, we'll have to build a much bigger jail to hold all the perverts she's knockin' out."

"There's something funny going on here, Chief. Has this woman some ulterior motive? I mean, what's in it for her? She can't be fucking everybody's brains out just for the hell of it, can she? Maybe she's after something, maybe she's got a plan."

"A plan? What kind of plan?"

"How do I know? Maybe she's going to start a counseling service for victims of satyriasis and she's building up a supply of customers. Think about it, Chief. People don't usually do things for no reason, it's not normal."

"But she's not people, she's a spirit out of somebody's dream."

"So? She could still have a motive, couldn't she?"

"If she does we don't know what the hell it is."

He was right, of course. We didn't know anything about her, but I had a growing suspicion that all was not strictly kosher here and I resolved to keep an eye peeled to see if I could ascertain some reason behind her behavior.

I ate dinner with Ellen at Woo's and when we walked back to Main Street I saw several dark vans with governmental seals on their sides whip past us and slide to a halt in front of the City Hall. The doors opened and a lot of guys piled out wearing flak jackets and berets and carrying Uzis. They vanished into the City Hall.

"What the hell is that all about?" I said.

"I don't know, but I'll bet you're going to find out," Ellen said drily.

"You don't mind, do you?" I said. "I'll never get that Pulitzer if I don't stay on top of things around here."

She smiled and said, "No, go ahead. I wouldn't stand between a man and his Pulitzer."

So I left her standing there and sprinted across the street to the City Hall and ducked inside. The Chief and a bunch of cops were in the squad room with the new guys who turned out to be the FBI special squad Agent Skinner had requested earlier. Skinner was briefing them.

"We don't know what she is or who she is or what the hell she's doing here in Midvale, gentlemen, but we do know she's knocking off the local citizens in bunches. Her modus operandi? She fucks their brains out."

A murmur swept the crowd, eyebrows shot up, a stirring passed through the ranks.

"That's right, gentlemen, you heard me," Skinner continued. "Chief Hawes here claims she's a succubus, a spirit who appears in men's dreams and has sex with them. So far she's nailed twenty-five men and everyone of them has ended up without brains."

One guy raised his hand and Skinner nodded at him.

"Question, Figgs?"

"Why don't they just arrest her?" Figgs said.

"We tried that," Chief Hawes said. "Trouble is, she's got some kind of strange power that clouds men's minds. One look at this lady and nobody can think straight until she's out of sight. Every guy ends up thinkin' with his donniker because she puts the whammy on them."

"But if nobody can even look at her, how are we going to do anything to her?" Figgs persisted.

"That's what we've got to find out," Skinner said. "We need a plan, some way to get at her without risking more lives. Any ideas?"

There was a long pause while everyone looked at his neighbor and racked his brain for a workable plan and after a moment a voice in the back said, "Why not use guys who aren't vulnerable?"

Everybody looked in his direction and Chief Hawes said, "Like who? We just said nobody can resist her, guys can only think of pussy when she's around."

"So get guys who don't like pussy," the voice replied.

"Out with it, Crandall," Skinner said. "What are you driving at?"

"Gay guys," Crandall said. "She can't turn on gay guys because they don't like women anyway."

"Jesus Christ, that might work!" the Chief said.

"Hmm," Skinner said. "Well done, Crandall. Good thinking. Crisp and to the point. Now, as I see it, we send in a squad of gay agents and..."

"Uh, sir, the Bureau doesn't have any gay agents," a voice said.

"Oh," Skinner said. "That's right. Chief, could you let us have a squad of gay cops?"

"What gay cops?" Chief Hawes demanded. "We don't have any gay cops here. This is small town America and everybody knows there aren't any gay guys in small town America. You want gay guys, go into the city where they hang out."

"No offense, Chief," Skinner said. "Okay, I say we get a busload of gay guys from the city and give them rooms in the hotel. When she tries to fuck their brains out and they turn her down flat, maybe she'll be so frustrated she'll leave town on her own."

"And if she doesn't?" the Chief said.

"Then the gay guys can overpower her with main force and bring her in."

"Uh, most gay guys don't like force, sir," another agent said.

"Pick the ones that do," Skinner said. "Figgs, take six men and go to town, rent a bus and fill it up with gay men and get them back here as fast as you can. Put them all on the payroll."

"Yessir," Figgs said. He quickly chose six guys and they hurried out. Skinner faced the remaining agents.

"Okay, gentlemen, we play a waiting game," he said. "Join Chief Hawes' men on surveillance. We keep her pinned down till Figgs get back. Any questions?"

There was none and the agents filed out and moved to their posts. Skinner left to confer with some other agents and the Chief and I repaired to Brady's where we ordered a pitcher of beer and fell to smoking cheroots.

"Think this'll work?" Hawes said.

"It could. Women don't mean a whole lot to the average gay man, you know."

"Yeah, maybe she's never even seen a gay guy before. Maybe nobody's ever got a whiff of her pheromones before without turning into a big dick and runnin' amuck after her."

"What have we got to lose? Nothing's worked so far, might as well give it a try. We've never seen her work her magic on a gay man so we won't know what happens till we try it."

"Yeah, if it doesn't work we just go on to plan... what, E?"

"Who knows?" I said. "I've lost count."

"Me, too," he said glumly.

We finished off the pitcher and the Chief went back

to the station while I mingled with the crowds standing around the hotel and I saw the first news media crew, a truck from a network station in the city. I wasted no time making hay in this first burst of media sunlight. I moved in on the guy with the mike.

"I'm Jack Grogan from the Beacon," I said. "I'm the one who broke the story."

"Grogan!" the guy exclaimed. "Great! We were looking for you. Hey, Ralph, get the camera over here. We got Grogan!" He lowered his voice and leaned in confidentially. "Is she for real, Grogan? No bullshit? This isn't a PR scam, is it?"

"She's real," I said. "When you see her you'll know she's real, all right. This is without doubt the sexiest woman on the planet Earth. This woman raises hard-ons on dead men. One look at her and the whole world turns into a giant pussy and your libido puts the rest of your brains on hold till she gets out of sight."

The poor sap was already caught up in the wonder of it all at the mere thought of such a creature. He licked his lips nervously and blinked two or three times and glanced toward the hotel which housed this phenomenon. The cameraman jostled his way through the crowd and jolted him from his reverie.

"This the guy, Bob?" he asked.

"Jack Grogan, ace reporter," I said.

"Yeah, this is him," Bob said. "Let's roll some tape here. You ready, Grogan? Just give us a rundown on the lady, you know, how many guys she's laid, how you know she's a succubus, shit like that. Okay?"

"Shoot," I said.

Ralph switched his camera on and Bob fired off his

first question and the first on-the-spot live report on Midvale's succubus went on tape for the eleven o'clock news. I cannily stressed her beauty and sexuality and left them dying to get a glimpse of her so they could see for themselves. I also stressed the spirit angle since people love mystery and hype and I knew it was going to be a sensation on TV because Bob was literally drooling when I cut him off after three minutes or so.

"But where did she come from, Mr. Grogan?" Bob pleaded on camera. "Have you spoken to her? Does she...?"

I stopped him. "I'm doing a day-by-day account of the whole story," I said. "I'm just entering into negotiations for a series of articles with one of the major newspaper chains and people can get the details there."

"But...!"

"If you'll excuse me, I have to meet with Chief Hawes and Mayor Grimes. Now that the FBI has been called in, we've got to forge a new plan for dealing with what could be one of the greatest threats to mankind since the invention of the atom bomb."

It was beautiful. I knew people everywhere would be hanging on my every word and desperate to learn more about so alluring a creature as our succubus. I also knew I'd soon be besieged with offers from The Times in L.A. and New York and everybody in between for exclusive coverage and that my journalistic future was secure. That Pulitzer was almost as good as mine.

Actually, there was no meeting since our latest plan was still unfolding and we didn't have any idea what our next one would be if the present one failed. I went in the front door of the City Hall and out the back and swung around and started for the Beacon. The place was a whirlwind of activity with Amos and Marti manning the phones while Bert barked orders to the printers and Art banged away on his computer.

Ada was fending off a clutch of news seekers at the front counter and she scowled at me. "How about some help over here, Grogan?" she said. "Give these guys some news so they'll get the hell out of the office."

"Folks, everything's under control, the FBI is..." I started to say and the crowd drowned me out with indignant cries and open threats.

"I want that woman arrested this minute!" one mighty pissed housewife screamed in my face.

"Somebody said she's after little boys now!" another shouted.

"You're not telling us the truth!" a third yelled. "She's an ogre with magical powers and Midvale is doomed!"

"It's all your fault, Grogan!" someone else sang out.

"Why blame me?" I said. "I only work here. You got any complaints, take them up with the FBI. In fact, go see Agent Skinner, he's at the police station and he's running the investigation. Tell him I sent you."

The mob turned as one and high-tailed it for the police station to revile Skinner for a while. Bert threw a handful of copy at Art and turned to me. He had a glint in his eye that was put there by a mixture of journalistic excitement at the prospect of a scoop on a really big breaking story and a kind of capitalistic glee at the thought of the windfall profits.

"It's big, Grogan," he said, "Real big. The story's on the wires, everybody's got it. New York called, Chicago, everybody. The networks are rushin' in camera crews, we already got fourteen pages of ads for tomorrow's extra..."

"It's bigger than you think, Bert. There's a Pulitzer in this thing. You hear me? The Beacon'll have a Pulitzer before we're done."

"Copy!" Bert said distractedly, looking around as though expecting it to pop out at him. "We need Marti on it. Tell them to crank out anything they can about the succubus, what their friends say, their parents, whoever. Send Art out for some on-the-street interviews. I'll knock out some filler on succubi and start a follow-up piece on our attempts to arrest her."

And that's what we did. Everybody worked his ass off until after midnight and on Friday morning we put out the first extra edition of the Beacon since the Confederates fired on Fort Sumter. We ran off ten thousand papers for a town with that many people and sold every damn one before noon. It was a journalistic first for the Beacon and Bert wore a grin so wide I thought he'd run afoul of the succubus and had his brains fucked out.

The circus really hit Midvale that Friday. There were TV crews from all of Christendom—and some from heathenistic states, as well—and reporters swarmed like ants. People from nearby towns drove over to see the succubus and each one of them had a camera around his neck and an expectant look in his eye. The Tonopah Rotary came en masse and posed in front of the hotel for group pictures and the local marching band put on a concert at dinnertime.

Every hotel and motel in town was booked by Monday morning and they stayed that way throughout the whole affair and beyond. In fact, people paid such high rates for rooms that everybody who had a bed and a kitchen to make breakfast in opened a bed and breakfast and went into the tourist business. The only rooms left in Midvale were in the Midvale Manor, but they weren't available.

Business everywhere boomed. Luigi's sold out for every meal and the line at O'Rourke's Wendy's went all the way around the corner and never got any shorter. Brady's had to add two more bartenders and the local bowling alley stayed open twenty-four hours a day to accommodate all the bowlers who poured into town. Actually, there weren't all that many bowlers, but there just wasn't a helluva lot more to do in Midvale than bowl, drink, eat, and gawk at the hotel.

And even I prospered. By Saturday morning I'd made a deal for a series on the succubus with the New York Times and was already on a first-name basis with the editor. With any luck there'd be a movie deal, maybe even a screenplay.

I was on the brink of an enormous success and it felt good.

Anyway, Saturday afternoon Agent Figgs showed up with a whole busload of gay men he'd collected in the city. As they came from the bus, I remembered his instructions to get some that could deal with force if necessary and apparently he'd had some luck in that area because a lot of these guys were buffed Mr. Americas and looked capable of beating the crap out of Arnold.

Maybe they'd be able to handle these sex-crazed spirits after all. They were ushered into the squad room and Agent Skinner briefed them.

"...so we came up with a plan. What we need is somebody who is invulnerable to her charms, somebody who can resist her pheromones and keep his mind on the right track. Well, gentlemen, that's where you come in. Since you're gay you aren't attracted to women, there's no so-called chemistry there.

"So what we'll do is put you in rooms at the hotel and the succubus is sure to make her move. When she shows up to fuck your brains out, you'll be unmoved by her sexuality and can tell her to get lost. We think she'll be so frustrated and pissed at being rejected that she'll go back where she came from and Midvale—and possibly the country—will be saved. Any questions?"

A guy down front raised his hand and said, "If she's a spirit, maybe she can change herself into a man. What happens then?"

"Don't worry, she can't do that."

"But what if she can?"

"Then you'll get your brains fucked out," the Chief said. "Any more questions?"

Another hand went up. "Is she really that good?" the guy asked. "Is sex with her so good it actually destroys men's minds?"

The Chief nodded soberly. "She's the best lay in the whole world," he said, and a buzz ran through the room as each man imagined himself on the receiving end of the best lay in the whole world.

Astonishing.

The briefing over they were led across the street to the hotel while hundreds of onlookers watched with bated breath. Marched inside, they were assigned to rooms on every floor and front to back so they were spread out more or less evenly. They were told to slam doors and flush toilets and play TVs so she'd know they were on the premises and the cops withdrew to await results.

It was still afternoon and we didn't expect any real action until nightfall so I went back to the Beacon and sorted through the mounds of messages which had already poured in. There were calls from all parts of the known world offering advice on how to catch and tame succubi. Every truck driver, lumberjack, ex-jock, construction worker, and pseudo-macho asshole in America wanted to come to Midvale and "nail this bimbo's ass to the floor" for us.

One guy, a Prof. Jaczlok, called three times from Austria and claimed to be a world-renowned expert on succubi male and female and averred he could rout her for a mere million dollars and expenses. I ignored them all, though, since it was out of my hands now that the feds had taken over. What the hell, I had Pulitzers to worry about.

I worked on my series for The Times until dinner and then Bert, Amos, Art, and I went to eat a celebratory dinner at Woo's and Bert generously picked up the check. After dinner I went home and stopped in at Andy's for a fast game of nine ball and found the place packed with strangers who were in town for the succubus. Laughter and crude jokes sounded in the murky air and the comforting click of pool balls click-

clicked on all sides. I decided to forgo the game and ended by having a beer and some conversation with Nick.

"She's still got us by the balls, eh?" he said

"Aptly put, Nick. A real stranglehold. And the feds are just as screwed up as we are. If this latest ploy doesn't work they may never get her out."

Nick shrugged. "They could always call in the army."

"Send the army against her? Shit, they wouldn't have a brain left among them if they tried that. This babe's supernatural, like she came from another world or something. No mere man can stand against her."

"Huh, the way I heard it, she makes all the guys stand."

"Oh, yeah, that way, but not on their own two feet."

Nick nodded at the pool players crowding the tables and said, "Maybe we should see if she's got any friends. I haven't had this many people in here since Minnesota Fats played an exhibition in '78."

"It's the sex. People like sex, even the ones who never get laid. Everybody wants a look at the sexiest woman in the world, a woman so sexy she can actually fuck a man's brains right out of his head and turn him into a sex maniac overnight."

"I don't blame them; I'd like to see her myself."

"You'll see her soon enough, everybody will. At the rate we're going, she'll have laid every guy in Midvale before the year's out and we'll all be idiots."

"You think those gay guys will pull it off?"

"Personally, I wouldn't bet on it. So far everybody

with balls has been rendered helpless at the sight of her or knocked out by inhaling the pheromones. Wouldn't surprise me if these guys ended up with IQs lower than sea level by dawn tomorrow."

"Might be worth it," Nick said somberly. "A guy gets laid by the sexiest woman on Earth and all it costs him is his brains. Lots of men make worse deals."

"She must be one incredible experience, all right," I said.

We lapsed into silence and reflected on that thought for a minute, then I went upstairs to my place and took a shower and laid down for a second to rest my eyes and when I woke up it was nearly eight o'clock. I went out to see what was happening with our succubus and stopped in at Lola's and found the place was filled to the gunnels with reporters and TV people. Being an ardent capitalist, Lola cunningly raised her prices and thereby extorted a small fortune from the visitors while considerately charging her regulars the usual rate. Small town people look after their own.

Chief Hawes and Carl were in a booth and I joined them. "Any news?" I asked.

"Nope," the Chief said. "Lola sent them over some 'burgers and fries and pea soup for dinner and the guys said nobody'd seen any sign of the succubus."

"Some of the braver ones even went up and banged on her door and dared her to come out and turn them on," Carl said, "but she never showed herself."

"We might be on to something here," I said. "Could be she knows she's out of her league and she's lying low."

"Or she's plannin' some outrage," Chief Hawes

said.

"Yeah," Carl said. He looked nervously around and looked ready to make a run for it if she suddenly popped in.

We adjourned to Main Street and lounged around with six hundred or so other people who were all waiting to see the outcome of the battle between the succubus and the gays. Ed Peters, the local bookie, was offering odds of five-to-one in favor of the succubus but few bettors took him up since most of them had already seen her and they remembered what she'd done to them.

The evening slipped away uneventfully and the crowds thinned out until only a hundred or so were still stationed in front of the hotel by eleven that night.

I'd been moving from the Beacon to the police station to the mayor's office and back again throughout the evening and finally decided there'd be no news until morning. I dropped by Ellen's but she wasn't home and I ended up at Andy's again.

This time I managed to shoot some nine ball with Nick and then we sat on some folding chairs by the counter and drank beer from the cooler and smoked a couple of cheroots. It was a pleasant interlude, one made almost spiritual by the thick cigar smoke, lighted tables, and deep shadows of a pool hall where Minnesota Fats had once played an exhibition.

I went up to my place about midnight and slept the untroubled sleep of innocence and awoke at seven sharp and was having some coffee and a cruller when I heard the sound of running feet and excited shouts outside my window. I jumped into my shoes and tucked in my shirt as I moved and headed for the action.

I sprinted along Elm and rounded the corner on Main and saw a crowd forming up in front of the hotel. A dozen or so of the gay guys were lining the sidewalk and others were emerging from the hotel and each time another one came out the crowd oohed and aahed and shook their heads and clicked their tongues and with good reason. It was clear that not a single one of them had a brain left in his head.

Chief Hawes was there lining up a bunch of squad cars to haul the latest casualties away to the booby hatch and I went up to him.

"Jesus Christ, Chief," I said, "what the hell happened?"

"Beats me, Grogan. All I know is what I see. You can't rely on gay guys to corral a succubus. She changed the whole bunch into a lot of straight heteros."

And damned if it wasn't so. The ex-gay guys were standing around wearing wacky grins and quantities of Old Spice. Each one also wore a substantial bulge in his pants and leered lasciviously at any remotely sexy female in sight. It was an amazing spectacle, one that would live in infamy in the gay world and henceforth be known as the Great Midvale Massacre.

CHAPTER FIFTEEN

The Succubus KOs The Special Squad And Plan E (or is it F?) Is Laid

An hour later the last of them had sidled out of the hotel and into waiting squad cars as a hushed crowd watched in dismay. Forty-six young men had not only had their brains fucked out but had simultaneously undergone a complete sexual reorientation and seen their lives changed forever. Incredible.

After the last squad car took the last load of ex-gays away, the crowd turned ugly and began excoriating the Chief for his failure to deal with the succubus. They demanded action and angry threats to "take things into our own hands" and "get us a Chief who knows what he's doing" filled the air. I edged away from the Chief and sought to dissociate myself from him since I saw no need for both of us being lynched, but the succubus herself diverted the crowd.

As the angry crowd closed in on the hapless Chief, the Rolls-Royce woman suddenly appeared in the doorway of the hotel and she was a sight to behold. The woman was wearing a shockingly revealing dress that was cut to her navel and slit up the thigh and so skin tight it seemed to flow over her unbelievable boobs and the voluptuous thighs that had so recently embraced forty-six erstwhile gay men. She dripped sensuality and clouds of pheromones could be seen hovering around her as she faced the throng.

On seeing her the crowd pulled back as one and a gasp went up from them and a few choked cries rang out in the stillness. As usual, every guy there was rendered hors de combat at the first glimpse and stood gaping at her with the punchy look of the ineffably aroused. The brazen hussy walked down the steps and onto the sidewalk and started along Main Street with disdain and arrogance while the entranced crowd was drawn inexorably after her.

At one point she suddenly stopped and turned around and the crowd lurched backwards and dozens of people were knocked down like bowling pins and a minor panic ensued, but she just smiled and resumed her journey. As she reached the corner, Agent Skinner and his squad of special agents raced up in their specially marked van and skidded to a stop. The agents poured out wearing their flak vests and determined expressions on their faces, but determination quickly gave way to slaphappy grins and stout erections as they got a good look at her.

The succubus smiled a devastating smile that caused those closest to it to come unhinged sexually and reach out for the nearest boobs and thighs and the owners of said boobs and thighs reacted by beating the crap out of the reachees, which only added to the confusion. She moved languidly to the special van and sat in its open door and slowly raised both legs and swung them into the van.

The vaunted special squad followed her in like a pack of dogs on the trail of a bitch in heat and when they were all inside the door was slammed shut and the van began rocking and bouncing and shimmying and teetering this way and that as cries of sheer delight and joy mixed with anguish and even pain filled the air.

The crowd surged forward, eyes bulging and nostrils flaring, and watched breathlessly. After some minutes the van stopped crashing about and an eerie silence settled over the scene as the crowd leaned in expectantly. A moment later the door opened and the succubus stepped out and gazed coolly at the onlookers as she tucked an errant boob back into her top and pulled her dress down over her thighs. Her eyes glistened in the morning sunlight and she ran a sensual tongue over her lips as she moved off.

It was too much for an old farmer named Jones. The poor bastard's ticker quit on him and he fell dead on the spot, but when he fell he landed on his back and an enormous hard-on pointed skyward and drew admiring glances from several nearby ladies. The succubus continued on her way and disappeared around the corner as Chief Hawes and I regained our wits and moved to the van to see if there were any survivors.

As we reached it the special agents started coming out and every one had been reduced to an intellectual cipher. They wore the telltale grins and were disheveled and screwed-up generally. The Chief looked at them and signaled for Wally Hicks who was standing nearby.

"Load them back in the van and take them to Doc Bane," he said, and Wally and some bystanders rounded up the agents, reloaded the van, and took off for the hospital while the crowd, overwhelmed by the display of raw power they'd just witnessed, fell back and began to disperse in haste that bordered on the unseemly.

We were back to square one. Every scheme we'd tried had failed utterly and the succubus had just knocked off forty-six gay guys and a dozen special squad FBI agents for a total of almost eighty men. If she kept this up Midvale would soon be the center for sexually depraved idiots. Something definitely had to be done, and done fast.

Eli, Carl, Chief Hawes, and I met at noon in the mayor's office to decide our next move. Even though it was a Sunday the place was crawling with media people looking for stories and irate and scared citizens milling about stirring up trouble. We ordered sandwiches from Lola's and ate lunch on the job to expedite matters.

"...Marines, by God!" Eli said. "They could get a thousand men and attack at dawn and blow her ass to smithereens."

"Eli could be right," Carl said. "This calls for drastic action. It's a cinch we'll never get her out of town by ourselves."

"How about if we send in a SWAT Team?" the Chief said.

"Midvale doesn't have a SWAT Team," Eli said.

"Oh, yeah, that's right," the Chief said. Then, "What if we used a sniper? We could put some cops up on the City Hall roof with rifles and when she comes out of the hotel we could riddle her ass like a Swiss cheese."

"No good," I said. "How would that look on the

national news? A beautiful and defenseless woman is shot down on the street because a lot of country bumpkins can't keep their peckers in their pants. We'd be the laughingstock of America and somebody would probably be indicted for murder or worse."

"Grogan's right," Carl said. "No snipers."

"Then we get the goddam Marines!" Eli said.

"We don't have to do anything," I said. "The networks have already reported on what happened to the FBI special squad and the whole country knows we've got a succubus here. We're going to have troops in Midvale whether we want them or not."

Just then the mayor's intercom buzzed and his secretary said, "The governor's on line two, Mr. Grimes."

Eli hit the switch on the speaker phone and said, "Hello, Governor, what can..?"

"What the hell happened to my aide?" The governor's angry voice snapped and crackled out of the box and Eli jumped back in alarm.

"The succubus got him," I said.

"What succubus? What the hell are you talking about?"

"We tried to tell him, Governor, but he wouldn't listen so she fucked his brains out," Carl said.

"You mean my aide doesn't have any brains?" the governor bellowed.

"Governor, she also got a dozen FBI agents and forty-six gay guys since last night," I said. "It might be a good idea if you roused the National Guard and sent them down here."

"Are you crazy?" the voice bellowed. "You want

me to mobilize the National Guard and spend millions to capture one woman? You forget this is an election year? How the hell am I gonna explain that to the voters? Listen, Grimes, you do something about that two-bit whore and do it now, understand? I don't want any more publicity, this shit could cost me the election if you keep screwing around down there."

We looked at each other and sighed in unison. "It's too late, Governor," I said at last. "Maybe you'd better come down here and take a look for yourself. Midvale is national news and there's nothing we can do about it now, election or no election."

"Jesus Christ," he said, "I'm surrounded by a bunch of incompetents. I want something done, I gotta do it myself!"

The line went dead and we all leaned back and looked at each other. "If he wants a miracle, he should call Lourdes," I said.

"You think that's what we need?" Carl said. "Divine intervention?"

"Hey, that's it!" I cried. "An exorcist! We need an exorcist!"

"What exorcist?" the Chief said. "We already tried that when we sicced Rev. Skaggs on her ass and look what happened to him."

"But he wasn't a real exorcist," I said. "That imbecile didn't know what he was doing. A real exorcist uses chants and smoke and incense and all kinds of magical charms and whatnot. Look, how did they deal with succubi in the Middle Ages? They called in an exorcist and he drove out the evil demons and made them run off with a lot of pigs."

"Yeah, like in that movie," the Chief said.

"Where are we gonna find an exorcist?" Eli demanded.

"Just call the church," I said. "They probably keep them on file."

"Why not?" the Chief said. "Give Fr. Rafferty a call and see if he's got any unemployed exorcists hangin' around."

Eli looked at his watch. "He's holdin' mass now. Mass ends at one."

"I'll stop by and see him myself," I said. "I'm going by the church anyway."

"Go for it," Eli said.

"Yeah," Carl said.

So I did. The meeting broke up and I headed out to St. Mary's on Spruce.

As I went down Main I saw a second wave of feds coming into town as two buses full of stern-visaged FBI agents trundled past on their way downtown. More grist for the succubus' mill, I thought. Mass had just ended when I got there and Fr. Rafferty himself was going up the walk to the rectory. He was an old codger just barely on the right side of eighty with a great shock of white hair and watery blue eyes that wandered in all directions in a seemingly endless search for something endlessly lost. I called to him and he turned around.

"My name's Grogan, Padre. I'm with the Beacon."

"Of course you are," he said. "Everybody knows that, you know."

"Padre, we need your help. It's about the succubus."

"Aye, I knew you'd come to me sooner or later, Mr.

Grogan. You need an exorcist now, don't you?"

"Aye, uh, I mean, yes, but how did you know?"

"Because you've got yourself a succubus and there's only one way to deal with a succubus, my friend. Exorcism. You have to meet the creatures head on and hit them with a dose of Latin and holy water, that's the only way to drive the demons out."

"Can you do it?"

"Of course I can do it. I've read up on the subject, I have. Come inside and I'll give you some Irish coffee and we can talk about it, lad."

We entered the rectory and I was surprised at the opulence of the place. There were good original paintings on the walls and ornate furniture and Oriental rugs everywhere, and all of it glossed over with a patina of quiet thoughtfulness and style. I couldn't help but comment on it.

"You live well, Padre. Exorcism must pay handsomely."

"Oh, it's nothing special, nothing at all. Just a few Hoppers and a Reginald Marsh or two mixed in with the odd Eakins or Bellows. I'm just a poor parish priest, you know. If you want opulence, go call on the bishop. Now there's a man of substance. First-rate art and the best of wines and brandies, and a houseful of antiques to boot."

We passed through the house and into a large, wood-paneled study with floor-to-ceiling bookcases full of leather-bound books that looked like someone had actually read them in recent times.

"I take it bishops are paid even better wages than exorcists then," I said.

"Yes, indeed, but not nearly so well as cardinals. Cardinals are the moguls of the Church, the ones who set the tone for the rest of us. A cardinal always lives in a mansion; it's required by canon law, you know, and he's bedecked with jewels and honors befitting a true Prince of the Church."

A pretty young thing entered then and said, "Yes, Father?"

"Two Irish coffees, please, Maureen."

The girl smiled and left and the good Father moved to an elaborately carved desk and picked up a burnished walnut humidor and flipped it open to reveal a box of Corona-Coronas—and Cuban yet! I helped myself to one of the fifteen-buck cigars and vaguely wondered why I'd never heard the call to the religious life.

The pretty Maureen returned with our coffee and I launched into my tale of lust and passion.

"About this succubus, Padre," I said. "She's already done in more than eighty men to date and has her eye on the rest of us. If we don't stop her pretty soon, she'll turn this town into a depraved pit of iniquity full of morons and sex maniacs. We've tried everything from force and cunning to magic and evangelism without success and we haven't got a single viable idea left. Then we remembered that when succubi flourished throughout Europe in the Middle Ages it was the Church that was called in to deal with them. And so we decided what we needed was an exorcist and that's why I'm here."

"You've come to the right place, my friend," the padre said. "I'm an authority on expurgating succubi and similar demons and devils. I've studied all the great masters in the trade, you know, and I've learned their secrets well. I've yet to meet the succubus who could stand against my charms."

"Fantastic. You'll save Midvale and the town will be forever grateful."

"And poorer, too. There's the matter of my fee."

"Name your price, Padre. After all, how much can mere money matter when the fate of an entire town is at stake?"

"But first, about this succubus. You say she attacks men at all hours of the day? Not just at night?"

"That's right. She got most of her victims at night, but she also knocked off an entire FBI special squad on Main Street at nine o'clock on a Sunday morning."

"Hmmm," he said, reflecting. "That's not like your average succubus, you know. Generally, they come only at night, and only in dreams at that. I've never heard of one of them actually appearing in the broad daylight before." He puffed thoughtfully on his cigar. "And you say Rev. Skaggs' cross and Bible routine had no effect on her at all, eh?"

"None. Eight minutes after he entered the room he was a brainless idiot."

"Yes, well, Skaggs was a brainless idiot all along, but that's another story."

He fell silent for a moment, then said, "All right. My fee will be a mere trifle. I'll rid Midvale of the succubus for a painting."

"A painting?"

"Yes. I understand Hopper's Early Sunday Morning is for sale. It's a bargain at only $1,000,000."

"Sold!" I said, "You don't come cheap, Padre, but

they say you get what you pay for. How soon can you start?"

"Right away. I'll lay in a fresh supply of holy water and begin choosing the proper Latin nouns and adjectives and start after her by noon tomorrow. You'll have to clear the area, no men within a block of the hotel. An enraged succubus under siege can be a dangerous adversary, you know."

"Don't worry, she's half way out of town already."

Satisfied that we had the succubus on the run at last, I went back to the mayor's office to report my success and organize the final assault.

CHAPTER SIXTEEN

Of the ACLU, Spaceships, And Exorcism

City Hall was swarming with feds by the time I got back there at two o'clock. The FBI had a command post set up in the mayor's office and the CIA had taken over the courtroom. Three choppers full of Marines in full battle gear landed in the City Hall parking lot and took up positions around the hotel while three busloads of state troopers ringed the hotel behind the Marines. Big searchlights were moved into position on all sides of the building and the streets were cordoned off with wooden sawhorses and flashing yellow warning lights.

From all the activity and ordinance in view, you'd have thought they had King Kong himself trapped on the roof.

I stopped in at Brady's for a beer and the place was packed with media types and feds of all kinds. They knew me by sight now and I found myself surrounded by inquiring minds demanding to know everything.

"Where did she come from?" one demanded.

"What's she like up close?" another said.

"Yeah, is she as good as they say she is?" a third chimed in. "Can she really fuck a guy's brains out?"

I signaled for a beer and leaned against the bar. "She's the ultimate lay," I said. "To get laid by a succubus is to experience the best sex there is anywhere. Words can't describe it; in fact, her victims can't even tell what happened to them. It's so good it completely discombobulates them and renders them mental eunuchs with hard-ons that won't go away."

The women present stared in wild-eyed wonder and one of them said, "Their hard-ons won't go away?"

"That's right. She turns them into moronic sex maniacs who can't think of anything but getting laid. They end up memorizing copies of Penthouse and trying to peep under ladies' skirts. Oh, it's a sad sight to see, all right. Poor wretches. That's an awful way to go through life."

One old lady in the back said, "Humph! Isn't that the way most men go through life?"

We ignored her, though, and a photographer who'd been shooting pictures the whole time stopped and said, "Why don't the cops just shoot her ass?"

"Because they can't," a tall guy wearing a cheap suit and an unkempt beard sang out.

"Oh, yeah?" someone else said. "Who says so?"

"The ACLU, that's who," the cheap suit said.

"I was wondering when you guys would show up," I said. "I suppose you're going to make a speech about the succubus' civil rights or some such shit."

"You damn right I am," he retorted. "Just because she's a spirit or even a demon or a witch or whatever the hell she is, she's still got rights and we're gonna see those rights are protected under the Constitution."

"But she's a ghost!" someone cried out. "Ghosts don't have any rights."

"We'll see about that," the ACLU guy said. "I'm

filing an injunction in the morning to restrain the police from harming this poor woman or from interfering with her basic rights to go and come as she pleases and live a life free from harassment of any kind."

"Who's harassing her?" I said. "We're the ones being harassed around here. Look what she did to the FBI's special squad. A dozen men rendered nincompoops and packed off to a mental ward because this woman assaulted them in the course of their duty. Who's looking after their rights?"

"Besides, the Constitution doesn't say anything about ghosts," another guy called out. "It says 'all men,' not spirits from the fourteenth century. I say they should just zap the bitch and get it over with."

Some shouted agreement while others argued for the succubus and in no time the place was bedlam as everyone took sides. I finished off my beer and half of another guy's who was busy arguing with his neighbor and made for the door.

Carl and Eli were in a small conference room since the feds kicked them out of the mayor's office and I told them about the ACLU guy.

"Yeah," Carl said, "the bastard says he'll file a class action suit on behalf of all succubi and other-world beings and sue us till hell freezes over if we don't cease and desist at once."

"Can he do that?" Eli said.

"Hell, yes, he can do that. What's more, he'll probably win and she'll get four or five million bucks from the town treasury. We'll have to raise taxes to pay off the judgment."

"You tell folks they have to pay extra taxes on

account of this succubus and they'll run her outta town on a rail and piss on this ACLU guy as they go by," Eli said.

"And they'll run you and me out right behind her," Carl said. "A lot of people are already blaming us for this whole mess. You'd think she was on our payroll."

"You guys are forgetting our exorcist," I said. "Fr. Rafferty claims she's duck soup, and he looks like a guy who knows his business. I've got confidence in him."

"Are you kiddin'?" Eli said. "He won't stand a chance. Why, the man's almost eighty years old and he doesn't know diddly squat about sex. She'll blind him with pheromones and..."

"He says he can do it." I said, interrupting. "Should I tell him to forget it? Do we have another plan? I mean, if somebody's got a better idea..."

"What do I care?" Eli said. "Let him try—but make him sign one of those releases first, Carl."

"Don't worry, I've got it covered."

We lapsed into silence and each of us stared vacantly into the middle distance and sighed inwardly as he felt the inexorable pressures of entertaining a twenty-first century succubus. Who would have thought that an excess of pudenda could cause so much trouble?

I went out on Main and idled away some time talking to feds and Marines and reporters and then ambled over to the Beacon where I did some work on The Times piece that was doing so much to help make the succubus the talk of the country. Talk show hosts included her in their monologues, film clips appeared on every newscast, doctors discussed learnedly of the condition of her victims, theologians rambled on about her significance vis-a-vis Thomas Aquinas' Summa Theologica, and a renewed interest in the spiritual world was sweeping the land. All in all, the lady had put Midvale—and me—on the map big time.

I stopped by Lola's for a 'burger and fries and ran into Ezra who joined me at my table. He looked around furtively and said, "They came back again."

"Who came back?"

"You know who. Aliens. I saw them. They hovered over my woods for ten minutes. I figured they were lookin' around, scoutin' the place or somethin.'"

"Big ship?"

He nodded. "Bigger'n a freight car. Red lights on it. I think they're comin' back again pretty soon."

"What makes you think so?"

"'Cause that's what they did before. They come one night 'n kind of hover over my farm 'n then a couple nights later they come back. That's what they did when that lady in the hotel came out drivin' that big car."

I sighed and chewed on a French fry. Ol' Ezra was losing it. Next thing you know he'd be going for spaceship rides and telling little green men stories all over the place. Still, he meant well and I humored him.

"What's she after, Ezra? What do you think she wants in Midvale?"

"They're takin' over, that's what I think. It's just like in 'The Invasion of the Moon Men,' they're lookin' for a weakness 'n when they find one they work on it till we're too weak to defend ourselves. Aliens do that all the time, you know."

"Yeah, well, you keep an eye out, Ezra, and if they come back you let me know, okay? Maybe we'll do a story in the Beacon."

"Oh, they'll be back, all right," he said, "they always come back."

He nodded knowingly and left. I polished off my 'burger and decided to round things out with a wedge of Lola's home-made apple pie a la mode and another mug of mocha java in spite of the muffled cries from my arteries and adjourned to the sidewalk to savor an after-dinner cheroot.

Just as I applied match to cheroot I saw Bill Swigert coming toward me. He was wearing a pair of binoculars around his neck and the remnants of the slaphappy grin on his mug. I noticed he was staring hard at a passing brunette clad in shorts and halter but I must admit that wasn't too singular since a half dozen other guys were watching the same girl with interest. In fact, I gave her the once over myself.

"Evening, Bill," I said.

He tore his eyes away from Miss Halter Top and looked at me with the shifty-eyed look of the guilty. I saw he was carrying a supply of girlie magazines in a plastic bag and one of those little toy telescopes with pictures of naked girls in them, which he peered into at regular intervals. He also had a suspicious bulge in his pants. It was a sad spectacle.

"You want to see some centerfolds?" he said. "Miss June's a dandy. So's Miss April. And Miss March..."

I admired each as he unfolded them and said, "They're all dandies, Bill."

"Yeah." He peered wistfully into his telescope and

then back in the direction of the by now vanished halter-top girl. And then he suddenly seemed to come to and a rational look popped into his eyes. "I like your stuff, Grogan," he said briskly. "You're a good writer, you make those stories zing." He leaned in. "I think you'll have this hotel thing whipped in no time, don't you?"

And with that he was off down the street looking for all the world like his old self. He even walked with a jaunty step that could only spring from a sense of well being—and yet he was brainless. Remarkable.

I wandered over to the hotel and saw Fr. Rafferty busy setting up for his onslaught on the succubus on the morrow. He was directing some guys in hoisting a barrel up on a jury-rigged kind of scaffolding over the front door while another crew was placing an eight-foot crucifix in a stand on the sidewalk and laying out a display of candles that smelled strongly of incense even before they were lit. A bunch of onlookers watched with interest and commented on his chances for success.

"Won't do no good," one said shaking his head.

"Naw, he won't have a brain left in is head this time tomorrow," another remarked.

"You can't stop her with a lot of mumbo jumbo," a third said. "You need a ten ton tank, that's what you need."

And so on. Frankly, I wasn't all that optimistic myself as I watched the priest work. He was a frail guy, a man one could describe as effete. Still, he was the self-styled expert on succubi so I figured he knew what he was up against.

All this time the feds were lying low and laying plans. Even though they'd taken over the operation, they had no viable scheme of their own so they let us go ahead with the good padre's exorcism while they hatched a plan. The Marines and state troopers kept the hotel surrounded but that was a delaying tactic at best since the succubus could saunter out at any time and paralyze every manjack of them with a glance and do with them as she would.

Anyway, I walked down Main to Ellen's office and she was there with a client. I waited out front until he left and then I went in.

"Unlike hookers, you guys always work on Sundays," I said.

"Oh, hi, Jack," she said with a nice smile I was beginning to look forward to seeing. "Maybe I should have been a hooker then. Sunday's our big day. I haven't had a Sunday off in five years."

"Well, take off the rest of this one. Let's go have a drink and make plans for tonight."

"Oh, we have plans for tonight, do we?"

"Not yet but we're working on some. Come on, we'll drive over to Tonopah and take in a movie or something."

"That's the best offer I've had all day. Wait till I freshen up a bit and I'll be ready to go."

Tonopah was double Midvale's size and it offered more in the way of a night life, but it still wasn't exactly Manhattan. We caught a movie that was listed as a comedy but looked like it was put together by a committee of undertakers and went to a club where scantily clad girls did their best to create an atmosphere of sin and debauchery without much success. Finally, we went back to Midvale and my place where we had a good deal more success in sin and debauchery on our own.

Ellen stayed over that night against my better judgment since such practices inevitably deepen any relationship and encourage expectations to rise, but I was glad she did, anyway. She was good company and I liked having her around even if it meant treading on dangerous ground.

We had breakfast at Lola's and Ellen went to her office while I lingered over a third mug of coffee with Art who stopped in on his way to the Beacon.

"She's still in there, I see," he said.

"But not for long. Fr. Rafferty says he'll have her out by dinnertime."

"Not according to Ed Peters. He's laying twenty-to-one on the succubus now."

"Any takers?"

"Are you kidding? Even the bishop's betting on the succubus. In fact, I heard two priests over in Tonopah have already applied for Fr. Rafferty's job."

I sighed and said, "It's a bitch, all right. She's one tough lady."

"She's not all bad news, though. Look at how business is going since she showed up. We've got a press run of twenty thousand for today's edition, that's two papers for every person in town. Bert's even thinking of turning the Beacon into a daily."

"Why? Once she's gone this place'll be as dull as it ever was. All the media will split and there'll be nobody left in Midvale except the same farmers and dullards who've always lived here. Bert'll be lucky to sell out the usual two editions."

"You're probably right. Midvale isn't exactly Las Vegas, is it?"

"Hell, it isn't even Akron or Toledo. Without the succubus this burg is just another jerkwater town on the way to nowhere. Still, it'd be nice if we could keep a little of the glamour, wouldn't it? Maybe even attract some new people and keep some money circulating."

"It'll take a miracle," Art said. "Midvale was a goner when they decided to run the freeway through Tonopah instead of here. People won't drive twenty miles over a two lane country road just to stop in a place like this."

"But just get yourself a bona fide succubus straight out of the fourteenth century and presto! the tourists pour in by the thousands."

"It's too bad most of them are carrying guns and wearing flak vests, though," Art said.

"Their money's good, too," I said.

"I guess so."

We gazed out on the throngs already up and about on a Midvale Monday morning and counted our blessings and we both thought: What the hell, enjoy it while you can.

Art and I went to the Beacon after breakfast and touched up our stories for the day. Bert came in and said they were bringing in a network newscaster to cover the succubus live and in person on the six o'clock news and a battery of Congressmen was coming in hoping to get their pictures on network TV. Eli was right, it was turning into a circus just as he'd said it would.

About eleven-thirty I moseyed out onto Main Street to see how Fr. Rafferty was coming along and found huge crowds standing around in an expectant silence. Some nuns were gathered in the street in front of the hotel and each was armed with a heavy crucifix and an incense lantern. A half-dozen altar boys wearing their church duds stood by with buckets full of holy water and a bullhorn and speaker system was readied on the sidewalk.

Fr. Rafferty was guiding a truck as it backed up to a first-floor window. It had a generator on it and a hose-like attachment that was hooked to a blower affair. I climbed over a sawhorse blocking the street and went up to him.

"What's with the blower, Padre?" I said.

"Incense. Succubi can't stand incense, you know. I'll smoke her out. We hook the hose up to that incense burner and pump it into the hotel. When she comes out I'll drop that barrel of holy water on her." He pointed to the barrel suspended over the door. "Then I'll hit her with a fusillade of Latin and the nuns will finish her off with a blast of Hail Marys."

"And what happens to the succubus?"

"She goes back where she came from, that's all. You can't kill a succubus, you know, since they're not alive to begin with. You can only drive them away with prayer and holy water."

"That's good enough," I said. "Let her go haunt some Austrian village or medieval castle somewhere just as long as she gets the hell out of Midvale."

"You'd better stand back here, son," he said. "We're getting ready to turn her on."

I moved back to the barricade and stood next to Chief Hawes where he was watching the proceedings.

"Odds are fifty-to-one on the succubus now," he said.

"Fifty-to-one? Maybe I should get in this myself."

"It's easy money."

The priest cranked up the generator and a rush of hot incense shot through the hose and the sudden burst of energy caused it to pop from the window and thrash about like a writhing snake. It spewed a cloud of incense over a knot of people standing nearby and they were instantly overcome with remorse and converted on the spot to Christianity. They immediately renounced the outside world and dedicated their lives to doing good works and trekked off to join monasteries and nunneries.

Fr. Rafferty grabbed the writhing hose and jammed it back through the window and the blower shot huge bursts of concentrated incense into the building. Once the hose was secure the good padre returned to the doorway and took up his position there. He bedecked himself with beads and palm fronds, took a hearty swig of holy water, raised a bejeweled crucifix, and began calling out loudly in Latin.

Tension mounted as the incense began filling the hotel and seeping from windows on the upper floors. After about ten minutes the succubus suddenly appeared on the small balcony overlooking Main Street and she looked down at the crowd. A slow smile spread across her face and she disappeared into her apartment.

A minute or so later there was a stirring in the crowd

and then the succubus was standing in the doorway with the same cool, calculating, seductive smile and people went nuts. As usual, all the guys were out of it on first sight and the women hissed and growled deep in their throats and glared spitefully at her.

Fortunately, Fr. Rafferty had very poor vision and he never really saw her, but he knew she was there from the reaction of the crowd. He bravely advanced toward her with the crucifix aloft and surrounded by a veritable cloudburst of Latin. The succubus went to meet him in single combat and when she reached the front door one of Fr. Rafferty's aides cut the rope and the barrel of holy water tipped and spilled all over her.

As it turned out, that wasn't a good idea. She was wearing a very thin cotton dress sans undergarments and the water made the clinging dress all but disappear and left her gorgeous body exposed to the world in all its glory. Every guy in sight headed toward her and they surged forward against the Marines and state troopers who still had their wits about them because they hadn't turned to look at the succubus.

Fr. Rafferty started forward himself and was almost close enough to see her and thereby put himself in jeopardy when he slipped on the holy water soaked concrete and fell heavily to the ground. Before he could right himself, the succubus laughed and started for him when all of a sudden a dozen angry nuns flew at her in a rage and drove her back into the hotel under a barrage of Hail Marys and vicious swings of their heavy crucifixes.

The succubus safely out of sight, several of us

regained our senses and moved in to rescue the fallen priest. I helped him up and saw that he was wild-eyed and shaken, his hands trembling, his head spinning.

"Fr. Rafferty, are you okay?" I said.

He looked at me and said, "That woman is no succubus!"

"It's okay, Padre, she's gone. You're safe now."

He looked about with terror-stricken eyes and said again, "The creature is not a succubus, I tell you. No succubus could possibly survive a barrel of holy water, but she only laughed. I don't know what she is, but she's no succubus!"

The Marines helped him off to a waiting ambulance and the people stood around muttering among themselves and glaring at the feds and cops and me, too, for that matter. I remembered I had a new installment to write for The Times and went back to the Beacon so I could start on it forthwith.

CHAPTER SEVENTEEN

Trouble Doubles With New Revelations

Things went downhill fast after the succubus routed Fr. Rafferty. For one thing, the entire event was played on the network news shows at six o'clock and it stirred up the whole country. Religious nuts said she was the anti-Christ and started giving their stuff away and running around looking for high hills where they could be picked up by some archangel or other and a band of satanists claimed she was the Devil and the cops arrested them for dancing naked in the street and acting like a lot of assholes.

A group of feminist protesters came by in a bus and began parading around with signs reading, "Free the Succubus!" and "Succubi For a Free Society!" and "Succubi Have Rights Too!" and so on. I might add that they got theirs a day or two later, but that's getting ahead of my story.

The mayor went on national TV and admitted we'd failed utterly in every attempt to stop the succubus and he said if anyone out there had any ideas he should give him a call. As an added incentive, he suggested the town council would be very generous in rewarding anyone successful in getting the job done.

Almost at once the lines were flooded with calls from every half-wit in the country with sure-fire ways to rid the town of succubi. One clown even suggested getting a guy with a flute à la the Pied Piper.

What was worse, though, a succession of people showed up personally to do the job and claim the reward. A guy who claimed to be Haitian came in at dinnertime and said he'd run her out of town with black magic. He set up some candles and made a look-alike doll and sat it on a little altar he'd put up on a card tale. Then he got some chickens and a rabbit or two and slit their throats and splashed blood all around and stuck pins in the doll and chanted a lot of nonsense while a crowd of onlookers watched. Finally, he pulled a kitten out of the box and prepared to slit its throat and a mob of pissed-off cat lovers beat the shit out of him on the spot.

We had the first of a continuing run of macho guys who were sure they were man enough to handle any woman and they all left minus their brains. One enormous black guy showed up and said, "Man, show me where is the bitch, you need a black man with a real dong. Ain't none of you amateur white fuckers knows how to handle a real woman. Look outta my way an' let a real man show this bitch where it's at." Fifteen minutes later he had the IQ of a gopher and was clipping centerfolds from Playboy.

And so they came. People lined the streets until midnight as these and other would-be heroes worked under the glare of floodlights and provided the tourists with entertainment. They cheered their favorites and booed some others and watched each of them lose his head over pussy. I hung around until midnight before heading for home and Ellen who was spending a second straight night at my place. Yeah, I know it was reckless of me, but she seemed worth the risk.

About four a.m. my phone rang and it was Ezra. The spaceship had come back just like he said it would and a guy drove off it in a Jaguar. I was pissed. I didn't get back to sleep for an hour.

Ellen and I had breakfast at Lola's at nine-thirty the next day and the Chief came in wearing a concerned look on his face.

"What's up, Chief?" I said. "More trouble?"

"You could say that," he said. He sat down and signaled Lola for coffee. "She went on a rampage last night. Caught a platoon of Marines in their sacks and fucked every last one of them. Almost fifty guys."

"Holy shit!" I said

"All in one night?" Ellen asked incredulously.

"That's not all. She's got a friend now."

"Another succubus?" I said.

He shook his head. "Not a woman, it's a guy. An incubus. Came in this morning, the handsomest goddam guy you ever laid eyes on. Big with blond hair and a face that looks like it was chiseled outta goddam granite. He pulled up in a Jaguar and when he climbed outta his car the women..."

"A Jaguar?!" I said. "He was driving a Jaguar?"

"Yeah, that's what I said," the Chief said testily. "Anyway, the women go gaga over this guy. They were tearin' their clothes off and throwing bras and panties at him, for Christ's sake. He went in the hotel and Mrs. Watkins and the Dorsey twins followed him in and ten minutes later they came out." He paused, sipped his coffee, blotted his mouth with his napkin. "They had their brains fucked out."

"What?" I said.

"Oh!" Ellen said.

"We took them over to Doc Bane's and he said it's just like the guys. Big, silly grins and no brains. What's even worse, it turned them into nymphos. Doc left the room for a minute and when he got back the Dorsey twins were in the sack with a squad of the Marines she got last night."

"Jesus," I said and started up.

"Where're you goin'?" the Chief said.

"Uh, I've got something to do and, uh, I'll be back." I started out and turned to Ellen. "I'll see you for lunch, Ellen. Your place." And I was on my way to Ezra's farm.

Ezra had a nice farm out on Forbes Road, eight hundred acres complete with cows and those big silos where they store wheat or something and the usual rusted art work in the fields. His house looked like something you'd see in a Currier and Ives print and it had a TV satellite dish on the roof. Another plutocrat farmer I thought, as I pulled into the circular drive.

Ezra came out of the house to meet me and I knew he'd been waiting because you just don't find these farmers lounging around the house at ten-thirty in the morning.

"Thought you'd show up..." he started to say but I interrupted him.

"What kind of car was it, Ezra? The one the guy was driving."

"It was a Jaguar. Just like I said."

"What'd the guy look like?"

"Um, let's see, he had blond hair and, uh..."

"Moustache? Beard? Long hair?"

"No, there wasn't any moustache 'n no beard, either. And his hair was kinda medium long."

"Where's this field where the spaceships land? Show me."

We got in Ezra's pickup and drove along a rutted path in the fields and skirted the woods for three or four hundred yards and took a right and there was the south forty. It was just a big field with a lot of weeds and crap growing in it.

We climbed out and walked through the field. Ezra pointed to some flattened weeds and said, "See there? That's where the Jaguar went. It drove out of the spaceship and right off the farm."

"Where are the tracks from the ship?"

"Ain't any. It never touched down. It kinda hovered just off the ground and there wasn't any sound or anything."

I couldn't believe it; I was absolutely stunned. I just stood there like a statue and looked at him. I thought I had the scoop of the century when I was dealing with succubi and suddenly I find myself looking at the scoop of the goddam millennium! Unbelievable!

"They're aliens, right?" Ezra said.

The sound of his voice brought me out of it and I was all reporter again.

"Look, Ezra, have you told anybody else about this?"

"Sure, lots of people. 'Course, none of them ever believe me."

"I believe you. Listen, keep this under your hat for now. Don't tell anybody else. I want Bert to get out an extra and you're going to be the star. You got a picture of yourself? One I can take with me?"

"Sure."

"Good. Let's go."

We raced back to the house and he gave me a picture of him standing near the barn with a pitchfork in hand. It looked like American Gothic without the lady. I sped back to town and into the Beacon like a man pursued by devils—or space aliens. I bolted into Bert's office so suddenly I scared the shit out of him and he was half way to the open window before he knew it was me.

"What the hell..!?" Bert said.

"Bert, they're aliens, for God's sake!" I said. "We need an extra, at least 50,000 papers and..."

"Who's an alien?" he said. "What the hell are you ravin' about?"

"The succubi. Both of them. They're not succubi at all, they're goddam space aliens from outer space. I know because he was driving a Jaguar..."

"The guy who came in this morning? The blond guy?"

"Yeah, that's him. Look, just get Al and Tom and tell them to gear up for a press run of 50,000 papers. Right now. Go on, call them."

Bert hesitated for a second and then he reached for the phone and told the printers about the extra. When he hung up I said, "Good. Now listen. Ezra Halley called me last night and said he saw another spaceship. It landed in his pasture and a guy came out of it driving a Jaguar. A blond guy. And this morning a blond guy drives up to the hotel in a Jaguar and all the women go nuts over him just like the guys do with the succubus, right? So I beat it out to Ezra's place and he shows me the tire tracks in the pasture where the Jaguar was." I stopped and looked at him for a moment. "Bert, they're space aliens and we're the only ones who know it!"

Bert was thunderstruck and it showed. He just sat there as though waiting for his brain to take it all in. Finally, he said, "Fifty thousand won't be enough! We'll double it!" He reached for the phone.

"All right!" I said. "Jesus, I feel like Orson Welles in '39! It's the Martians landing in New Jersey all over again!"

"We need copy," Bert said crisply. "And pictures. Get Art and Amos on it. Call Marti in. You write the lead story. We go to press in two hours."

Jesus, it was an incredible rush. I loved it. A big breaking story, a gigantic scoop, extras. Was there anything like it in the world? In minutes I was banging away on my computer and rehearsing acceptance speeches at the Pulitzer awards dinner.

Astonishing.

At one o'clock we loaded every available vehicle and sent them off in every direction with a 100,000 copies of the Beacon's second extra in a week. The headline screamed ALIENS IN MIDVALE! and pictures of the hotel and Marines and the female alien and Ezra's farm and interviews with guys fucked brainless and it was altogether the most beautiful newspaper I'd ever seen in my entire life.

But that was only the beginning. As we were still loading the papers in cars and trucks, the Chief came by to see me.

"Well, she did it again," he said glumly.

"She did what?"

"She fucked the Congressional committee. Every one of them. They insisted the feds give them a personal tour and they were lookin' in the lobby when she showed up and drew them on into the hotel like so many sheep. They're still in there, too."

"You mean she's got hostages now?"

"Looks like it."

"Great. Here, take a look at this." I handed him a copy of the paper and watched as he got the shock of his life.

"Jesus Christ, Grogan, you must be kiddin'!"

"I wish. They're real aliens, all right."

"And they just kidnapped a dozen Congressmen!"

And so they had. I followed the Chief as he headed back to City Hall to spread the word. The feds refused to believe us until I gave them the details, but I finally convinced them. Naturally, they wanted to post a complete blackout on the media but I saw that coming and headed them off at the pass by getting our extra out before I told them. I mean, I haven't been a reporter for fifteen years for nothing, you know.

Anyway, it was almost too late. The aliens teamed up and went on a fucking rampage. They came out of the hotel and everyone was instantly under their spell. All the guys turned into stiff pricks the minute they laid eyes on her and now every woman became a hot-blooded, panting and raving sexpot as soon as she laid eyes on the blond guy. It was a sight to behold.

I was on the sidewalk with Amos and his camera when they came out and we quickly looked away as soon as the crowd's reaction told us she was outside.

Amos got some pictures by aiming his camera in her general direction and firing away and I watched the scene obliquely, concentrating on the people and avoiding looking at her.

The two of them went out and poured pheromones into the atmosphere like a kind of sexual acid rain and men and women on all sides were overcome by passion and lust and they followed them back into the hotel like rats after Mr. P. Piper. In no time they'd made off with fifty or sixty more hostages right before our eyes.

Two hours later the story was all over the country and twenty minutes after that the whole world knew Midvale harbored aliens from space. The President ordered the army in and the sky was suddenly filled with helicopters ferrying soldiers this way and that and Air Force jets streaked back and forth across the heavens like huge angry bees looking for someone to sting.

A batch of generals landed in the City Hall parking lot around dinnertime and they took over the entire building as a command post. A ring of soldiers was thrown up around the whole town and entrance was denied everybody without special clearance. Every top reporter and TV newscaster in the country was in Midvale by nightfall and an anxious world waited breathlessly for news of the planet Earth's first bona fide space visitors.

As the one who'd broken the story, I was grilled by everybody with access to a grill. An hour after the generals arrived, I was called in for interrogation.

When I entered the mayor's former office I saw

so many stars I was momentarily blinded by their radiance. There must have been at least ten or eleven generals present with an admiral or two thrown in for good measure. The brass were led by General John Horatio O'Malley, a tough old bird who'd won world renown for his brilliant and fearless invasion of Grenada a few years back, and he was pissed.

"So you're Grogan, eh?" he said with a sneer.

He was off to a bad start; nobody sneers at The Kid, by God. "That's right. I'm a reporter and..."

"Who gave you permission to publish the story on the aliens?" he demanded.

"Nobody gives me permission to write, Colonel," I said. "I don't need no stinking permission; it says so in the Constitution."

"Do you know you could be charged with treason?" he fumed. "Do you realize you may have put the entire world in jeopardy just so you could get a goddam scoop for this rag you work for?"

Now I was pissed. "With all due respect, Major, why don't you go fuck yourself?" I said. "I'm not in the army; you can't do shit to me and you know it."

Well, the old coot flew into a rage and had to be restrained by his pals to keep him from beating the crap out of me on the spot. After he was dragged off to one side, another guy wearing three stars took over the interrogation.

"Now, Mr. Grogan," he said, "if it's all right with you, we would like to ask a few questions. After all, this is a very serious matter, the Earth may very well be in considerable danger and we need the facts before we can respond here."

"Okay, that's more like it. What do you want to know?"

"Everything."

So I told him everything. I told him how I first saw her in the Rolls and last saw her and her new-found friend paralyzing minds and kidnapping people a few hours ago. It was a good story and they hung on my every word, especially the parts where I talked about her unbelievable sexual prowess.

And who could blame them? What red-blooded American man, or any other breed for that matter, wouldn't drool a bit and run a tongue over dry lips at the thought of nailing the best lay in the history of sex?

I finished my story and nobody moved or spoke. Even O'Malley stared blankly at me from across the room. Finally, there was a collective stirring and somebody cleared his throat and somebody else coughed. Then three stars said, "You've been closest to this from the start, Mr. Grogan. Any ideas?"

I shrugged. "Nuke them?"

CHAPTER EIGHTEEN

Grogan Gets Photos And Ada Gets Nailed

They let me go then and I went back to the Beacon where Bert and Art were checking the books.

"We sold out, Grogan!" Bert said. "Every last copy, all 100,000 of them!"

"And we're gonna do it again tomorrow!" Art said grinning.

"Two extras in a row," I said. "You'll be building your own San Simeon if you keep this up, Bert."

"Damn right I will." He looked at Art and back at me and said, "You know what we need? A picture. A picture of them in action."

"You mean getting laid?" I said, astounded. "How the hell can we do that? You know what happens if we even look at this woman..."

"Not her, him," Art said eagerly. "A picture of him in action."

"That's right," Bert said. "You can look at him all you want. He only affects females."

"But how...?"

"We got it all figured out, Grogan," Art said. "All you have to do is sneak in the hotel and find him. Then follow him until he strikes again."

"Yeah, maybe you can get some shots of him and the hostages," Bert said.

"Are you crazy? What if I run into her? One false

move and I'd be sans brains just like the rest of them. I don't give a damn if you sell a million papers, I'm not interested."

"Say, why not take a woman along?" Art said. "That way she could deal with the female alien and you could handle the male."

"That's a good idea," Bert said. "Sort of like insurance."

"You're nuts," I said. "What woman would be crazy enough to go in there with two space aliens?"

"Ada," Bert said.

"Forget it, I won't do it. It's too risky."

"Oh, it's risky, all right," Bert said. "'Course, it'd make a helluva nice touch for the Pulitzer committee when they pick the next winner."

"What a story, Grogan!" Art said. He drew imaginary headlines in the air. "'Close Up—The Aliens.' Text and pictures by Jack Grogan. It'd be a natural, by God!"

"I don't give a damn, what good is a...?" I stopped when the word Pulitzer triggered something in my brain. A picture would be a nice touch, wouldn't it? Might even make the difference between a Pulitzer and second place. Hmm.

"How about it, Grogan?" Bert said.

"Okay, okay, I'll get a picture," I said finally. "But if I end up without any brains..."

Art handed me a camera. "Here. All you have to do is aim and press the button. It advances the film automatically."

"Go get Ada," Bert said. "We'll sign her up."

And so it was decided I'd invade the aliens' inner-sanctum and take pictures of them in action, but I was only doing it for art's sake.

I went out on Main Street and watched the Marines and odd guards as they idled at their posts and went over to Lola's for a cup of coffee while I waited for Ada to powder her nose and hose herself down with cologne.

Lola had a crew busy preparing dinner for the hostages and, incidentally, Midvale's uninvited guests. Rows of insulated containers were on the counter and people were filling them up with Lola's special spaghetti dinners complete with loaves of French bread and jugs of Chianti. Some feds were supervising the operation.

I downed a cup of coffee and went back out on Main Street and saw Ada coming toward me. I met her on the corner behind a squad of Marines manning the barricade there.

"All set?" I said.

"Damn right. These guys don't scare me."

"Now remember, if we meet up with the woman, you distract her so she won't get me. And if we meet the guy, I'll do the same."

"Got it. Now how do we get in?"

"Good question. We wait for an opportunity. Maybe..."

Just then the protest group that had been demanding freedom and justice for all succubi yesterday showed up with new signs demanding equal justice for space aliens. They rushed the Marines fifty strong and headed for the hotel with signs aloft and cries for aliens' rights. The Marines went after them and confusion reigned.

"Now's our chance, Ada. We'll slip in the back

way!"

We started around back as the confusion grew and people ran every which way and shouted contradictory orders and generally went berserk. As we rounded a corner, I looked over and saw the alien guy come out on the sidewalk and fire a salvo of pheromones at the protesters and the women threw down their signs and started after him showering the air with cast-off clothing as they went.

I knew the lady would be right behind him and they'd have fifty more hostages for us to deal with.

We scooted around back and ducked in through a side door near the receiving area and climbed the stairs to the first floor. I cautiously opened a door and looked out in the hall to see if the coast was clear.

"You wait here," I told Ada. "I'll scout ahead. If I'm not back in five minutes, you beat it and save yourself."

"Right," she said.

I slipped out and tiptoed along the hall toward the lobby. I made it to a door that opened into the lobby and I just started to open it when I heard someone coming. Whirling about, I spotted a door marked Linens and slipped inside. I closed the door but left a crack where I could peer out. A few seconds later the male alien hoved into view with a gaggle of women clamoring after him in various stages of undress and panting and sighing like a lot of lovesick teenagers chasing a rock musician.

The guy was a hunk, a regular Adonis. No wonder the girls went nuts over him. Tall and blond and square-jawed, he had a look in his eye that would have captivated Mother Teresa. They disappeared around the corner and I slipped out and went after them.

Rounding the corner I saw a door to a large conference room as it closed behind them. I approached the door carefully and cracked it open just a hair and gazed in on a scene straight out of a sexual fantasy land. The women had shed every stitch of clothing and they were all over him in a wild tangle of arms and legs and buttocks and boobs and pudenda. He was already hard at work fucking brains out right and left.

The women moaned and called out in the throes of ecstasy and writhed around and fought to be next as he rendered one of their colleagues brainless. He was giving a cute little blonde number what for and, out of her mind with sheer passion, she emitted a peculiar high-pitched cry as he finished her off. In a flash he rolled off and I caught a glimpse of his enormous donniker as it glistened briefly in the dim light of the curtained room before disappearing into a tall brunette who straddled it and went completely nuts in turn.

Everybody's mind was so clouded with pheromones and runaway libidos and an overwhelming desire to get laid herself that no one paid any attention to anything but the alien. I pushed the door open and fired away with the camera more or less blindly and then ducked out and sprinted back down the hall to where I'd left Ada. As I turned the corner on my way back I heard another commotion and slipped back into the linen closet again just as a crowd of guys entered the hall in hot pursuit of the female alien.

Fortunately, I didn't see her as she was somewhere in their midst and blocked from my view. After they'd passed, I stepped out and had to put a hand out to steady myself as I inhaled residual pheromones lingering in the air. Still groggy and confused for a moment, I made a wrong turn and headed back to the conference room. I saw a door and, thinking it was the one I'd entered by, opened it and went in.

As I closed the door behind me, I felt a hand on my shoulder and turned to find myself gazing into the faces of the Dorsey twins. They were naked as jaybirds and wearing slaphappy grins and a minute later I was being sexually assaulted by twin sets of female parts. Naturally, I resisted as best I could, but it was no use. The wanton creatures pulled me to the floor and in no time I was stripped bare and covered with naked girls.

After what seemed like an eternity, I struggled to sit up and assess the situation. The girls were nowhere in sight. I dressed hurriedly and went out and this time made the right turn toward the stairs to the basement where Ada was waiting. I reached the door when I heard the same high-pitched crying sound of a woman on the receiving end of the greatest fuck of her life coming from a nearby room. I listened at the door just as the cry dropped into the steady, soft moan of a woman now bereft of her senses and I knew it was all over.

I went back to the stairwell and hid until the door to the room opened and he came out and started down the hall. After he'd gone I went over and opened the door and there was Ada sans clothes and grinning to beat the band.

"Holy shit!" I said. "Ada! Are you all right?"

She beamed happily at me and her eyes sparkled saucily. I grabbed up her stuff and hustled her into her clothes but it was rough going because she took them off almost as fast as I could get them on. When I'd managed to get her more or less dressed, I opened the door just as a bevy of naked girls frolicked by with a lot of equally naked old fat guys. Apparently, Congress was still in session—or soon would be.

We made it back to the stairwell and through the basement without further incident even though Ada didn't want to go. She kept pulling back and muttering something about big sticks or bricks or something but I just told her to shut up and keep moving.

Once outside, we sprinted for the barricades and one mighty pissed-off FBI guy wanted know what the hell we were doing, anyway, but I ignored him and lit out for the Beacon. Bert and Art were waiting for us. They took one look at Ada and knew the worst.

"The bastard got her!" Bert said.

I steered Ada to a seat and she sat there with her hands folded in her lap and smiled contentedly all the while.

"I don't know what happened," I said. "I left Ada in a stairwell while I went to reconnoiter and the next thing I know the alien's fucking her brains out. It was over before I could do anything."

"Poor Ada," Art said morosely, but it almost seemed a wasted emotion since poor Ada appeared to be quite pleased with things.

"Did you get the pictures?" Bert said.

"Nice segue, Bert," I said. "Worthy of Hearst himself. Yeah, I got the pictures, or at least I think

I did. He took those protesters to the conference room and nailed every last one of them. You should have been there. It looked like a scene from a Bosch landscape or one of the levels in Dante's hell. Naked bodies everywhere, women moaning and calling out, and everybody half mad with desire and passion and raw lust. He went through them like Don Juan at a swingers' convention and turned them into a lot of empty-headed nymphomaniacs before you could say Jack Robinson."

I stopped but Bert and Art didn't. They were staring vacantly into space while imagining such a scene with themselves playing key roles. Mouths hanging open, eyes glazed and unblinking, donnikers rising, and all from a second-hand account of the action. After a moment, Bert snapped to.

"Uh, yeah," he said huskily. "It must've been awful."

Art blinked. "Yeah, awful."

I tossed the camera to Art. "Anyway, look them over. If they didn't turn out, too bad. I'm not going back in there no matter what."

Art grabbed the camera and started for the darkroom and Bert reached into his desk and brought out the bourbon. "Good work, Grogan. Have a drink. You probably need one."

I nodded at Ada. "Pour three glasses. She needs one, too."

So Bert poured three glasses and we sat down on each side of Ada and put an arm around her bony shoulders. She smilingly raised her glass in a toast and we touched glasses with hers.

"To success," Bert said.
"To fame and fortune," I said.
"To big tricks," Ada said, and she grinned broadly and winked at me and her eyes twinkled brightly.
Amazing.

CHAPTER NINETEEN

Abandoned

The presses were rolling an hour later and the Beacon's second extra in two days was on its way complete with two half decent shots of the carnage in the conference room. Of course, we had to place a few strategic black bars here and there to hide the exposed naughty parts since the Beacon is a family paper, but the pictures were startling, nevertheless. In fact, the whole piece was so dynamic and powerful I could almost see that Pulitzer on my mantel. Surely, I'd nailed the bastard down with this story.

After the paper went to press, I called Ellen and met her for lunch at Lola's. I filled her in on my experiences in the hotel but I left out the part about the Dorsey twins. What the hell, it wouldn't do any good and a lot of women get pissed when they find out you've been laying miscellaneous sets of twins on the side. Besides, it was all their fault, anyway.

"What about the hostages?" she said. "Can't they escape?"

"They don't want to. Hell, they haven't got any brains left; they like it there."

"How can the army get the aliens out as long as they have the hostages?"

"Good question. If it weren't for those Congressmen, they could just level the place, but everybody knows you can't go around rubbing out valuable politicians. Those aliens have nothing to fear as long as they've got a dozen U.S. Congressmen in there with them."

"They could starve them out."

"Can't do that, either. We have to feed the hostages, and if they eat so do the aliens."

"Then what are they going to do? Are we stuck with these creatures forever?"

"Beats me. Right now I'd say they're in the driver's seat."

Ellen frowned and reached to adjust a strap on her shoe and her gaping blouse provided an enticing view of her excellent breasts. I felt a spell of dizziness come over me and I reached out to steady myself and put both hands squarely on them. Ellen looked up.

"You've got your hands on my breasts," she said.

"I know. I must've inhaled some pheromones in the hotel. Let's go to my place."

"Now?"

"Yeah, right now."

Our eyes met and I thought I saw vagrant glints of light flickering in the depths of hers that hadn't been there before the aliens showed up. Jesus, maybe we were all being infected by their mere presence and the whole town was well on its way to becoming something else.

"Yes, all right," she said, her eyes fixed on mine.

So we went to my place and it was incredible. We were so turned on and blown away by it all that we fell together in a mad frenzy without even bothering to remove any more clothes than necessary to get the job done. Afterwards, we lay on the rumpled bed in utter exhaustion and fought to regain our strength and wits. Then Ellen said, "Is it my imagination or is it getting better every time we make love?"

"I don't know, but I'm not sure I can stand it if it gets much better than this."

She smiled and leaned over to kiss me.

Remarkable.

I went back to the Beacon after lunch and found Gen. O'Malley there along with three or four of his pals and he was pissed, as usual.

"There you are!" he snapped. "Does it take you two hours to eat lunch, Grogan?"

"Fuck you, Sergeant," I said.

He clenched his fists and turned beet red, but this time he managed to control himself. He held up a copy of the latest edition of the Beacon. "You took this picture in the hotel, didn't you?"

"Yep."

"I want to know what you saw in there."

"I saw a lot of naked people getting laid."

"Did you see the Congressmen?"

"Yep, they were naked and getting laid, too."

He turned to Bert. "I don't want that in the paper," he said.

This time it was Bert's turn. "Fuck you, Corporal," he said.

"By God, that did it!" O'Malley bellowed. "You can't talk to me like that! You guys are nothing but small town hicks and I'm a general in the United States Army, by God!"

"We don't care who you are, mister," Bert said. "Folks around here figure one man's as good as another and the Beacon does, too. Congressmen are news and we don't fix the news up so it won't offend people, not even for army generals. I'll admit a brainless Congressman isn't really news since there are so many of them around, but this batch is special. The story goes as is."

"I'll have the President declare martial law!" O'Malley fumed. "And I'll throw your farmer's ass in the goddam stockade when he does!"

He stormed out with his flunkies and Bert said, "Hey, can he do that?"

"Maybe he can. An invasion by aliens is pretty good reason to declare martial law, but don't worry about it. He's got bigger problems on his hands than a bunch of wise-ass reporters on a two-bit newspaper."

"What two-bit newspaper?" Bert said indignantly. "The Beacon's a first class..."

"I know it is, I'm just saying that's what he thinks, but he doesn't know we're about to win a Pulitzer."

"You're damn right," Bert said. He nodded and reached into his desk for the bourbon and I helped myself to a cigar from his humidor.

Now that word of the aliens had spread to every part of the globe, people were running amuck everywhere. The stock market tumbled and stockbrokers were leaping from tall buildings in a rerun of '29; people quit their jobs and got drunk or laid or stoned or all three; troops were called up worldwide as people girded themselves for imminent invasion by hordes of oversexed creatures from distant worlds.

What was even more ominous, though, was that the aliens stepped up their attacks on the local citizenry.

While guards surrounded the hotel at all times, the aliens were still able to move out into the nearby streets and assault new victims. In one such foray they teamed up to attack a banquet at the Midvale country club and before the night was over they'd laid and de-brained almost two hundred people between them. In fact, they added insult to injury by wiping out a whole platoon of airborne troops and kidnapping the commander on their way back to the hotel.

It was clear we'd reached a crisis but nobody knew what to do about it. The generals met in war councils and laid plans but none of them was any good.

Even though O'Malley didn't like us, he included Eli, Carl, Chief Hawes, and me in the planning because we were still the ones with the most experience in dealing with the aliens, but we weren't able to do much good, either, because we'd already done everything we could think of.

After the country club raid, though, people demanded action and the generals freaked out. A crowd of angry citizens stormed City Hall and threatened to drag everybody out and beat the shit out of them if they didn't do something and do it quick. O'Malley decided to take a long shot and rush the hotel with a full company of infantry and try to overpower them by sheer numbers, but it was a mistake.

They secretly readied 220 soldiers and moved them into position at the front and back entrances at midnight. At 12:06 a.m. somebody blew a whistle and the searchlights flashed on and bathed the area in light as the soldiers ran into the building with their guns at the ready. A crowd of onlookers—it was a top secret operation but everybody knew about it and showed up to watch—lined the streets and peered intently at the hotel as shouts and slamming doors and the sound of running feet echoed in the night. Then an eerie, all-encompassing silence descended on the scene and lasted for a full minute until peals of ribald laughter rose on the still night air and scared the shit out of everybody within earshot.

The laughter was followed by raucous partying noises as rock music, exuberant cries, and clouds of pheromones poured from the building in a crazy, sensual amalgam that drifted outward, fell, settled, and patined the people below with confused longing mixed with anxiety and half a hard-on.

The Midvale Manor was now SRO with mentally deficient libidinal lunatics taking up all available space. They took no new victims in after they got the infantry. People nailed after that were sent back out to grin and leer and further reinforce what the aliens were doing to us. The town had seen almost three hundred innocent men and women turned into lascivious, grinning, hedonistic, live-for-the-moment sex addicts who spent all their time in pursuit of each other and diversions generally.

And so it went. Gradually, those fucked brainless were becoming something different in more subtle ways. They smiled a lot, for example. They seemed upbeat, more open. Of course, they spent most of their waking time laying and getting laid in elevators and stairwells and cars and stockrooms and johns and fields and all over the place, but something more was going on, something beyond mere sex.

The strange fever also seemed to be spreading in some insidious way without direct contact with one or another of the aliens. For example, take Emma Demp. Emma worked at Finch's furniture store and was happily married to Bob Demp who owned a bump shop on Oak. Well, I was in Finch's one day and when I went to get a drink of water next to the receiving room I heard a heavy thumping noise over near the john. Curious, I took a look behind some crates and there was Emma stark naked and astride Billy the stock boy. One look at the anguish/lust/intensity in her face and I knew she was possessed and under the direct influence of the aliens.

Actually, I found out later she'd been banging Billy for months before the aliens even showed up, but the point's made just the same. The people of Midvale were undergoing a massive crisis, a moral and spiritual and emotional metamorphosis whose consequences could only be guessed.

In fact, it was fear of this subtle change that brought things to a head shortly after the loss of the infantry. Drs. Gramble and Bane had been following the victims closely and they were the first to notice the gradual changes taking place in people. Doc Gramble finally knew something was very wrong when he found himself banging Hetty Conn, his sexy red-haired nurse, on the examining table in his office. Chagrined, he turned himself in at once—as soon as he finished banging her, that is—to the medical board, but since there's no AMA rule against doctors banging their nurses he avoided censure.

Still, he knew it was an ominous sign and he

confided in Dr. Bane. Working together, they surmised that people were being contaminated by unseen pheromones and they alerted the authorities. Gen. O'Malley, mimicking Gen. MacArthur's famous flight from the Philippines, hied himself and his pals to safety outside the town and ordered Midvale sealed off from the rest of the world. No one could enter or leave without express permission from the generals for fear they'd carry this new disease beyond the town and infect the rest of mankind.

Naturally, this didn't sit too well with those left behind including yours truly, especially since the aliens began making more forays into the community and winning new converts by the score. The night the generals left the female alien hit the weekly poker game in Ed Beckett's barn and fucked everybody silly, and an hour later she popped out of a cake at Tommy Glantz's bachelor party and laid him and twenty-six celebrants in record time.

Tommy went ahead with the wedding as scheduled and his frazzled bride filed for divorce within a fortnight on the grounds of sexual incompatibility, which is to say he was fucking her to death. It turned out okay in the end, though, because the next day the male alien caught her in the backroom of Tisch's hardware where she worked and gave her what for on a roll of burlap. After that, she and Tommy were both seething sexpots and they got on handsomely.

Anyway, those of us left pondered our fate and looked for a way out. All the high muck-a-mucks had flown the coop with O'Malley but they'd left behind all the troops and feds who'd been here from the start for fear they'd already been infected and these guys were pissed, too. Eli got his office back and some of the army guys and feds began hanging around there with us.

A couple of days after the big pull out a bunch of us were in Eli's office scheming to come up with a new angle.

"I say we use snipers," Eli said. "Hell, we're in a war here, boys, we've been invaded just the same as if the Russians were landin' in the town square. We wouldn't hesitate to shoot Russians so why in hell can't we shoot space aliens?"

"Because they won't let us," Major Banks said. "Gen. O'Malley left orders not to harm the aliens. If we shoot them we'd be court-martialed or worse."

"Great, he runs for his life and says we shouldn't hurt anybody," Chief Hawes said.

"It's easy for him to say because he not in danger of getting his brains scrambled," Carl said.

"So we can't shoot them," I said. "Okay, forget that and think. Is there some other way we can get at them? Maybe drop a net over them or stun them with taser guns or..."

"We could gas the bastards," Carl said. "A little tear gas or a shot of nerve gas to paralyze them might do the trick."

"But what about the hostages?" the major said. "If you gas the aliens, you also gas them. I don't think it's a good idea to go around gassing U.S. Congressmen."

"Why the hell not?" the Chief said.

"The major's right, no gas," I said. "We'd have the Geneva Convention on our ass in no time and the

U.N.'d censure us before the whole world. We need something unique, special..."

I trailed off and we lapsed into a brooding silence. After a moment the Chief said, "Shit, it was easier when we were dealin' with the succubi. At least they're from this planet."

Bingo! A light went on in my head. I sat up so suddenly the others were startled and they turned to look at me.

"What?" the Chief said.

"You all right?" Maj. Banks said.

"Succubi," I said. "That's our answer. Look, these aliens are making mincemeat out of us because nobody on Earth can out-fuck them, right?"

"So?" Carl said.

"So nobody human can out-fuck them, but what about something nonhuman—like a succubus? Fucking people is their business, they've been doing it for centuries. If anybody can match the aliens in the sex department, it's gotta be a succubus."

"Yeah, so?" Carl said again.

"So all we have to do is find an incubus—and a succubus, too, since we need one of each—and turn them loose in the hotel. The aliens will jump them and get their own brains fucked out!"

"But where the hell are we gonna get a succubus?" Eli demanded.

"I don't know but I've got an idea." I rose and started out. "I've got a call to make."

I left and went to the Beacon and started rummaging through the debris piled around my desk and in less than ten minutes found what I was looking for.

I grabbed a phone, punched in some numbers, and listened impatiently as it rang.

CHAPTER TWENTY

More Losses—The End Is In Sight

Ellen stayed over again that night and it occurred to me that we were spending more time together than was recommended by the Bachelor's Guide for Maintaining the Status Quo but I didn't care. Maybe it was the pheromones.

We ate breakfast at Lola's, as usual. I had the steak 'n eggs special with a side order of grits and was just eating the last grit when Chief Hawes came in wearing a concerned look.

I said, "Don't tell me, the aliens fucked up the rest of Midvale last night."

"Close. They ravaged the old folks' home and skewered everybody in the place. Now they've got two hundred old-timers running amuck out there and carryin' on like a bunch of berserk lechers. I may have to run the whole crowd in for violatin' the state morality laws."

"Maybe the aliens did them a favor," Ellen said. "Yesterday they were sitting around waiting to die."

"Then they did the people in Lakeside Terraces a favor, too," the Chief went on. "All four hundred of them. The aliens hit every unit after they left the old folks' home, so Midvale's got four hundred new morons all grinnin' like Cheshire cats in heat."

"They got the whole complex?" I said.

"Every single one of them."

We looked at each other and Ellen said absently, "I wonder what it's like?"

"What what's like?" I said.

"To make love to him."

"The alien?"

She nodded. "I guess it must be something pretty special, mustn't it?"

"At the rate we're going, I'd say your chances of finding out are pretty good," I said. "If we don't do something soon, we'll all know what it's like. This town will have the lowest IQs in the country and the highest concentration of sexual deviants. We'll make Sodom and Gomorrah look like Sunday school camps."

"I thought you had a new plan?" the Chief said.

"I do, and I have to get going. I should be getting a call any time now."

"Who from?" the Chief said.

"The world's leading expert on succubi, a man known as Prof. Jaczlok. He's from Austria."

"But they're not succubi," the Chief said. "They're aliens from outer space. What good will a succubus expert do?"

I started up. "A lot, I hope. How about lunch, Ellen? Twelve-thirty?"

"Sounds great," she said.

Ellen went to her office and Chief Hawes and I started down Main Street together. He went to the City Hall and I kept going to the Beacon where Ada stopped me on the way in. She was wearing a short-skirt outfit cut daringly low and had an unmistakable glint in her eye that was proving too much for Farmer Cobb, an old geezer Ada was bedazzling over the counter. Her copy of Playgirl lay face up on the counter and I caught a glimpse of the centerfold as I drew near. Poor Ada.

"Hey, Grogan, there was a call for you. Man said it was important. The number's on your desk."

"Great, that's got to be the professor."

I found the number and called it. A military-sounding voice said, "Central Command. Lt. Higgins."

"I'm Grogan from the Midvale Beacon. I'm returning a call from Prof. Jaczlok."

"One minute, sir."

I waited for two minutes and then a voice came on the line. "Grogan?" it roared in my ear. "Did you know your town is surrounded by soldiers? And they're idiots, too. All soldiers are idiots, it's one of the requirements to be a soldier. I told them who I am but how can one talk to idiots? They understand nothing, they..."

"Hey, it's okay, Professor," I interrupted. "I'll fix it. There's a Col. Harris there. You've been cleared with him, just find him and tell him who you are. I'll see you at the Beacon, okay?"

"Yes, but remember, we're dealing with idiots so who knows?"

The line went dead. I hung up and went outside where I lit a cheroot and reflected on the vicissitudes of life while waiting for the professor to show up. Lola saw me standing there and she crossed the street and approached me.

"Hear about the mayor, Grogan? Aliens got him. Got Eli and Carl and everybody else in City Hall."

"What?! She got the mayor? He's brainless now?"

"He never was all that smart to begin with, you know."

"Holy shit!"

"That isn't all, either. She laid the whole fire department and her friend scored with every girl in the tri-county choir festival. Over two hundred girls. Seems there's no getting away from that pair. Every time I go in the backroom to get something I expect that bastard to jump out and screw me half to death in my own restaurant."

"Jesus, maybe we're already too late," I said, more to myself than Lola.

Lola nodded. "That's what a lot of folks are saying. This town will never be the same again, Grogan, 'cuz the people won't ever be like they were before."

More prophetic words.

She turned and retreated back across the street just as Barney's cab rolled around the corner with the professor in the back seat. He climbed out and stuck out his hand.

"Ah, you are Mr. Grogan," he said. "I know you are not a soldier because you don't look like an idiot."

"Thanks—I think. Welcome to Midvale, Professor. Come on in and we'll get you a cold drink."

We started in. Jaczlok was the stereotypical academic in a rumpled suit and disheveled mien but he still projected an air of confidence and efficiency.

God, I sure hoped he was efficient.

Once inside, he stopped and stared at Ada where she sat grinning behind the counter. She batted her eyes and crossed her legs and behaved shamelessly and scared the shit out of him. He drew back and half raised an arm in the classic defensive posture of someone fearing imminent attack. I took his arm and steered him to Bert's unoccupied office and got us a couple of cold beers.

He gestured in Ada's direction. "She is one of them, no? The alien has had his way with her?"

"I'm afraid so, Professor."

"Ha! I knew it. She is without brains. But that is not the work of a succubus. If succubi did that to us, none of us would have the IQ of a canary. We have all been ravished in our dreams by succubi, you know." He looked disdainfully at the glass of Bud he was holding. "Have you no Austrian beer? This is not beer, it is only pretending to be beer. Only we Austrians know how to make real beer."

"I'll send out for some..."

"Never mind. I have not come to drink beer but to save the world from an invasion of Martians."

"Truth is, we don't know where they're from but..."

"No matter. You say they behave like succubi. So. We fight fire with fire or, in this case, aliens with succubi."

"You think it'll work?"

"Why not? These creatures have no experience with succubi. Consider. The aliens adopt our form and use sex as a weapon to overcome us. Sex is a powerful emotion, they make it their strength. Maybe they use it as a way of controlling their own kind back on their home planet. So, they use it to control us. If we bring them together with succubi and the aliens are unable to conquer them, it is possible they will leave us for easier prey somewhere else in the universe. That is our plan, no?"

"That's our plan, yes. But are you sure the succubi can out-fuck the aliens?"

"Why not? They're spirits. How can anyone, human or otherwise, overpower a spirit who is by definition without form and therefore invulnerable? Our only problem is getting the aliens and succubi together."

"And how do you do that?"

"Succubi only appear in dreams and to dream one must be asleep. Therefore, we induce sleep by some means and the succubi will invade their dreams and the battle will be joined."

"But where are we going to find succubi?"

"They are already here. They are everywhere. And they love to be challenged. Have you ever noticed that succubi most frequently appear in the dreams of old-maid librarians and fundamentalist preachers? It is their sense of humor; they enjoy playing tricks on their victims. And we encourage them a little, too. We send romantic music into the hotel, strew fragrant flowers everywhere, bathe the building in candlelight, put erotic pictures on the walls and make such an atmosphere of sensuality, of lust that succubi will be sure to appear. Have no fear, as soon as the aliens sleep succubi will be there. But the aliens do not sleep, so how will we induce sleep?"

"I've got it. We've been sending food in since they got here and captured the hostages. Maybe we could slip some drugs or something into their food and knock them out that way."

"Then you also knock out the hostages, no?"

"So what? In fact, that's good. We could send people in there and rescue them while everybody's out cold."

"Hmm," he said. "Good, we do it like that. Who has drugs?"

"Kaz over at the drugstore. Come on."

We finished our beers and headed for Kaz's place. Kaz was dubious when he first heard our plan. "I can't go administering powerful sedatives to people without a prescription," he protested. "I could lose my license."

"You'll lose all your brains before the week's out if you don't," I said. "Besides, we don't need megadoses, just enough to knock out a few hundred people."

"Some barbiturates," the professor said. "Only enough to induce sound sleep for dreams."

"But I don't have enough for that many people," Kaz said. "I'd have to order a supply in and that would take a week at least."

"You could get some at the hospital," I said, "if you tell them it's to save the world."

Kaz agreed at last because he really didn't have much choice. Midvale was lost without immediate action and he knew it as well as we did. We left Kaz to line up the barbiturates and stopped by Lola's to tell her of our plan and to be ready to add drugs to tomorrow's dinner before it was sent to the hotel. Then I got the professor a place to stay so he could rest up a bit and I went to Ellen's office.

When I got there I saw the door standing open and something in the back of my head switched a little danger signal on. I stepped inside and there was no sign of her. As I stood there I heard a muffled sound and then the unmistakable high-pitched crying sound of a woman in the midst of the climax of her life and I knew at once I was too late.

I tried the door to the back and it was locked. Frantically, I kicked at it and managed to splinter it on the fourth or fifth kick and reached an arm through to unlock the door. Ellen was sprawled on the floor with her skirt around her waist and her blouse torn open and a familiar wild look in her eye as she lay there panting from the best sex of her entire life.

The alien was nowhere to be seen and I rushed to her side. "Ellen!" I cried. "Jesus, are you all right? Did he...?"

She looked at me coquettishly and cocked her head to one side and tried to pull me down to her. I pulled back and tried to straighten her clothing that she persisted in trying to keep unstraightened. I finally put her on the couch and got hold of Doc Gramble on the phone. He came over but there was nothing he could do.

"It's no use," he said. "I can't do anything. She's not hurt, just let her rest up. Get her a supply of porno stuff and maybe a set of dildos and she'll be pretty near her old self in a few days."

"'Pretty near' isn't the same as her old self, is it?"

"Nope, it isn't, but..." and he shrugged.

I took Ellen home and she absolutely refused to let me leave without making love to her, so I did and it was a remarkable experience to say the least.

She was an entirely new Ellen, wild and voracious and insatiable and multi-orgasmic and altogether fantastic.

When we finished she fell asleep and I looked at her with a feeling of remorse and loss because I knew I wanted her around for good and that was probably impossible now. I'd never be able to match her energy, never be able to truly satisfy her. I left in a blue funk and went back to the Beacon.

CHAPTER TWENTY-ONE

The Return of The Succubi

Time was of the essence now. We needed twenty-four hours to get our plan in motion because of the logistics involved in rounding up thousands of bouquets of fragrant flowers, stringing wires for speakers, laying hands on a ton of erotica, and getting a supply of candles for the romantic lighting required.

We worked at breakneck speed and still fell behind in our race with the aliens. They stepped up their horny wanderings and swept everything south of the water tower that night. They struck home after home, bar after restaurant after movie house, and left a small army of grinning sexaholics in their wake. The Chief and councilman Torpor were about the only town officials still capable of reasoning and old man Torpor wasn't too consistent even then. Even Doc Gramble was a common sight on the streets fondling his red-haired nurse and disgracing himself in public without apparent shame.

Unbelievable.

In brief, Midvale looked like a war-ravaged, besieged town in the last moments before the enemy hordes poured over the ramparts and put the place to the torch. Sandbag emplacements lined Main Street, the searchlights stood like sentinels, helmeted soldiers were everywhere, and a pall of pheromones and anguish and despair settled on everything and everyone.

The next day the professor took charge of setting up for the big fuck-off and I went to see Kaz. He was in the back mixing up a vat of barbiturates and wore a worried look.

"Jesus Christ, Grogan, I feel like a mass murderer here," he said as he dumped in another ten-pound sack of barbiturates and stirred it with a broken canoe paddle. "If the pharmacy board finds out about this, I'll be drummed out of the profession."

"Nonsense. You'll be given an award for outstanding achievement in the pill pushing trade." I peered into the vat. "How's it coming?"

"Don't get too close. The fumes from this stuff could put you in a deep coma."

"Will it be ready for dinnertime?"

"Yeah. I'll dry it into a powder and they can grind it up in the food. If they mix it evenly, every portion should have enough dope to put a man to sleep for at least eight hours."

"But will it put an alien to sleep?"

"How the hell do I know? I've never drugged an alien before. It should work, though. Since these guys took on human form, they probably react pretty much as humans do. I'd say a square meal of this stuff will have them sleeping like babies."

"And dreaming like frustrated old-maid librarians after watching a Johnny Dicke porno flick, I hope."

Kaz sighed mightily. "I sure hope we know what we're doing, Grogan," he said.

"So do I," I said. "So do I."

I went back to my place where Ellen was staying to see how she was doing and I found her in a flustered state with every sign indicating she'd either just entertained one or more visitors or she'd been trying out the new dildos I bought her. Whichever, it hadn't been enough and I was forced to submit to the most egregious sexual antics before she'd let me leave.

I was on my way back to the Beacon when I ran into Chief Hawes and Wally Hicks. They both seemed wearied, beaten men.

"You look like hell, Chief," I said. "And so do you, Wally. What the hell's going on?"

"We lost, Grogan," the Chief said. "It's all over. They knocked off the north end of town, went through them like Sherman goin' through Georgia. There's hardly a man or woman left in Midvale who can still think about anything except gettin' laid and havin' a good time."

"It's not just Midvale anymore, Chief," I said, "it's everybody. If we don't stop them here, they'll fuck the whole world up and we'll be slaves to some kind of intergalactic pussy. We can't quit now, not till we drive the bastards back to wherever they came from and save our country and the world from oblivion."

"Gee, it's like being in a John Wayne movie," Wally said.

"You better act fast, there aren't many of us left to fight them off," the Chief said.

A bevy of jet fighters swept over the town then and a helicopter swung in low behind them and headed for the City Hall parking lot. It had stars all over its sides.

"Visitors," I said. "Probably that asshole O'Malley

with some cockamamie scheme to save his own ass at the expense of ours. Let's go see what he wants."

We cut through the City Hall and out into the parking lot where the chopper had landed and we were right, it was O'Malley. He strode purposefully toward us while armed guards fanned out on either side on the lookout for sexually aroused space aliens.

"Where's Mayor Grimes?" O'Malley demanded.

"The last time I saw him he was memorizing Miss July and drinking margaritas at Brady's," I said.

"Well, who's in charge now? Where's Agent Skinner? Or Major Banks?"

"Fucked senseless, every last one of them. The only town official who can still think straight is Chief Hawes here."

O'Malley turned to the Chief and scowled.

"Okay, Chief, then I'll tell you. I've been in touch with the Pentagon and the White House. The President has called a national emergency and declared martial law for Midvale and put the town under my command."

"Then I suppose you'll be moving back in town to take charge of things?" I said.

"Uh, well, not exactly," he stammered. "That is, I'll run things from my command post outside the town limits in order to, uh,..."

"Keep from gettin' your brains fucked out?" the Chief said.

O'Malley glared at him.

"I'm putting the town of Midvale on alert. A wall will be erected around the entire town and a minefield laid for 500 yards on either side of the wall. Anyone trying to enter or leave Midvale will be summarily shot.

The town of Midvale is hereby designated a national hazardous zone and all its residents quarantined until further notice."

"So we're sacrificial lambs, eh?" I said. "You're throwing us to the wolves. Well, we'll see about that. I'll skewer your ass in the national press, I'll tell the world how you assholes abandoned us to an invading force and left us here to be picked off one by one. We'll organize national protests, picket the Pentagon, march on Washington, file civil rights violations and raise Cain..."

"Tough shit, Grogan," O'Malley said with a malicious grin. "You won't do anything of the kind because you no longer exist."

"Why, you arrogant sonofabitch!" I grabbed for his throat and the soldiers grabbed me by mine and held me back.

"Like I said, Grogan, you don't exist."

He turned and retreated to the chopper and it lifted off into the air. It made a low, mocking swing over the parking lot and sailed away.

"That's that, then," the Chief said, "we're goners now for sure."

"Maybe so but I'm not going anywhere without a fight."

I went back to the Beacon and found it abandoned by all except Ada who was entertaining Farmer Cobb in Bert's office. I went to my desk and rattled off a brilliant piece decrying the abandonment of an entire American town by a callous and indifferent government and dispatched it to the wire services.

That done, I crossed the street to Brady's and found

Bert and the entire Beacon staff watching porno flicks on TV and playing grab ass with each other. Topless girls were everywhere and sexual hi-jinks were the order of the day.

Appalling.

I had a double Scotch and managed to struggle free when two stark-naked women tried to drag me behind the bar. I went outside and saw Prof. Jaczlok supervising the unloading of huge mounds of flowers in front of the hotel. Piles of Playboy centerfolds, Sports Illustrated swim suit pictures, and posters depicting scenes from the Kama Sutra were stacked on the street ready to go up on the walls and a crew was readying dozens of speakers for the romantic music.

"How's it look, Professor?" I said.

"Good, very good. We are nearly ready. They have a nice dinner and a nice nap. We bring out the hostages and I call in the spirits and we watch and wait. Soon poof! it is over."

"If the succubi win, what'll happen to the aliens?"

"They will leave. If not, the succubi will give them no peace. You'll see, they will go back where they came from."

"That's too bad. I was hoping they'd go to Washington."

I left the professor to his work and went to Lola's to see how the poisoning was coming along. Lola was in the kitchen measuring out powdered barbiturates with a big hand scoop and tossing them into the split pea soup.

"One plate of this stuff and they'll sleep like dead men," she said.

"Watch it. We don't want them in comas, do we? Can people dream in a coma?"

Lola shrugged and said, "According to your professor out there, the deeper the better. He says spirits like to work in a nice, deep sleep."

"In that case, give them another shot."

I dumped a five-pound sack into the gravy and gave it a stir.

Since everything seemed to be under control, I went back to my place, took a shower, and lay down for a few minutes to collect my wits. It was like coming to the end of a roller-coaster ride, to the slow part just before the mile long upside down barrel loop and two hundred foot free fall final section and I had to get ready for it.

The town was about wiped out by now. Once the aliens got under way, they were sexual automatons with indefatigable organs that swept everything before them. I figured they were in a mopping up operation now and would be coming back for the ones they missed the first time around. It'd probably be all over by tomorrow one way or another.

I was worried about Ellen, too. She'd gone back to her place this morning and I wondered how she was doing. What the hell was I going to do about her? Was there anything I could do? And what happens to Midvale if we do drive the aliens out? The town wasn't doing all that well before, would it ever recover? Or would it turn into a ghost town complete with tumbling tumbleweeds and unhinged doors banging in the wind?

Jesus.

I put my shoes on and lit a cheroot and started out. It was nearly six and time to launch our final assault. Lola would be serving up individual dinners about now and stacking them in warmers and the professor should be ready to make his move.

I went outside and saw Abner King across the street in front of his haberdashery. He was hauling his inventory away in a dumpster and the sidewalk was lined with rows of pinball machines and video games for his new arcade. He supervised things with the familiar grin of the brainless fuckee while his wife brazenly flirted with the workers amid an atmosphere of gaiety and abandon.

I didn't know it at the time, of course, but this was only the start of radical changes that were sweeping Midvale even then. The die had been cast, the Rubicon crossed, the end foretold.

I found the professor sitting in an easy chair on Main Street with his feet up on a packing case of champagne. He had an open bottle on the sidewalk next to him and a crystal wine glass in hand.

"Ah," he said, "you are here. Good. Have some champagne. It adds a nice touch to an orgy, no?"

"Champagne would add a nice touch to a lynching, but do we need cases of the stuff?"

He handed me a glass and poured.

"It's for the succubi. A little wine is good for romance. We leave it in the hotel and they drink it and it relaxes inhibitions."

"Whose? Those aliens sure as hell don't have any inhibitions, and who ever heard of an inhibited spirit?"

"Trust me, Mr. Grogan, I know what we must do."

"Whatever you say, Professor. I'm getting to where I almost don't give a damn anymore."

Lola came out on the sidewalk and called down to us. "They ready to eat now?" she sang out.

"Yes, ready," the professor said.

"Okay, coming up!"

She disappeared back into the restaurant and Chief Hawes came out of the City Hall and joined us. I popped open another bottle of champagne and handed him a glass.

"It's for romance, Chief," I said. "Have some. Maybe you'll get lucky."

"Spare me. That kind of luck I don't need."

We drank the cold wine and stared bleakly across at the hotel. Occasional squeals of delight emanated from it and peals of laughter rang out as the hostages partied and screwed around. There was no sign of the aliens.

Lola came out pushing a big cart laden with warmer baskets full of dinners of mashed potatoes, fried chicken, split pea soup, and twenty or so pounds of barbiturates. The professor and I gave her a hand and we pushed the carts up to the hotel's front door and gave them a shove inside and unseen hands took over from there. We heard a clatter of cutlery and rattle of china and requests for someone to pass the hot rolls and knew we'd soon learn the fruits of our devious plan.

We had a couple dozen guys, mostly soldiers and some TV people, who'd also been overlooked by the aliens and could still function and they were assembled on Main Street to rescue the hostages as soon as they were rendered hors de combat by their dinner.

After about an hour an ominous silence filled the air. No laughter, no squeals of delight, nothing. We fidgeted nervously and sipped champagne and muttered among ourselves. I'd fallen into a brown study myself and pondered my own bleak future of lonely drifting from newspaper to newspaper in an ever increasing meaninglessness that would hardly be ameliorated even by a Pulitzer.

And all because a couple of sex freaks from interstellar space picked this town as a rendezvous for their annual let's-fuck-up-a-planet outing.

Maybe it was the champagne, or maybe it was the accumulated pheromones in my system, but suddenly I felt the vague stirrings of a plan forming itself in my mind. Maybe there was a way I could have it all even now, a way to have Ellen and my Pulitzer and a semblance of sanity, a way to avoid ever increasing meaninglessness.

My reverie was broken then when I heard the professor barking orders as the second phase of the operation went into effect. The men sprang forward and raced into the hotel to rescue the hostages and I followed them in. The place was littered with zonked out men and women in various stages of undress. They sprawled in lobby chairs, curled up on the floor, lay in heaps in the hallways, and snored away in rooms on every floor.

We explored tentatively and determined the aliens were out before we started grabbing people up and carrying them outside and across the street to the City

Hall where we stacked them up like cord wood. It took us almost an hour to carry the last one out and leave the aliens as the only occupants of the hotel.

When we had the last hostage out everybody dropped where he was and took a well-deserved break. The Chief came over and sat down beside me on the curb.

"Should we tell O'Malley we saved the hostages?" he asked.

I shook my head. "If he knew that he'd want to nuke the place. Let's see if the succubi work first."

"Wonder where the aliens went?"

"Who knows? They've probably gone to an oyster bar somewhere to recoup their strength."

"We better get movin' while they're out. They could come back any minute."

"You're right. Come on, let's go."

We roused the men and they grudgingly stirred themselves and began carrying flowers and champagne into the hotel. A crew began hooking up speakers and sticking lewd pictures and Kama Sutra posters all over the walls.

Flowers were draped over furniture and scattered through the lobby and in all the rooms until the place smelled like a huge six-story flower shop. Sexy colognes were sprayed around and bottles of champagne uncorked and poured into fluted crystal glasses as the first strains of a Sinatra ballad wafted through the building.

By eight o'clock we were just about ready. The professor broke open a case of candles and we made our last trip inside to add the final romantic touch by bathing the place with soft candlelight. Outside, pastel-tinted searchlights flooded the building in delicate shades of pinks and yellows and some guys on the roof dumped sacks of sparkling that landed on windowsills and stuck in the bricks and turned the building into something out of a fairyland.

Finally, Prof. Jaczlok brought out a card table and stood it up in the middle of Main Street. He placed a container of flash powder on the table, sat a pint bottle of a yellow-colored, watery liquid next to it, lit a small candle which gave off a peculiar odor as it burned, and opened a thin leather book with colored ribbons hanging from it that marked off certain pages.

He began reading from the book in some esoteric tongue and after a few minutes suddenly reached out and lit the flash powder which went up in a six-foot high burst of color and light. A moment later he snatched up the bottle of yellow liquid, opened it, and ran up and splashed it across the front of the hotel.

A heavy, musky aroma rose in the still, multi-colored air and slowly spread over the building.

That done, he sighed mightily and came back to the sidewalk in front of the City Hall and resumed his seat in his easy chair.

"That's it?" I said.

He nodded and gestured at the hotel. "No succubus can resist this," he said. "They will come."

Everybody settled in to await the arrival of the succubi and the return of the aliens. I stood around aimlessly for a few minutes, then the plan that had formed earlier resurfaced and I resolutely determined to do it, by God.

I slipped away in the gathering gloom and crossed Main Street as though headed for my place, but then I cut through the vacant lot across from Lola's and when I couldn't be seen by the others I ducked around to the back of the hotel and went in through the receiving entrance. I followed the same route Ada and I had taken earlier and made it to the door leading to the hall. I cracked it open a bit and looked out and was hit with the heavy aroma of hundreds of flowers and the soft glow of candlelight.

I entered the hall and made my way to the lobby. Nothing stirred anywhere. Sinatra's voice intermingled with the light and flowers and the place was truly transformed. I sat on a couch facing the lobby desk, picked up a glass of champagne and sipped it, then leaned back and settled in to wait.

I must have dozed off for a time and when I came to later I sensed a movement near at hand and looked to my left and saw the male alien watching me. I grinned at him and raised my glass in a salute and he smiled back and picked up a glass from a table and returned my toast. A moment later I felt rather than heard someone or something to my right and I looked in that direction. She was standing there in a shimmery black gown that hung in silken folds on her incredible body.

I was instantly mesmerized. My jaw dropped and my eyes bulged and I licked suddenly dry lips while she gazed coolly at me. She turned and moved off and I trailed after her as though attached by an invisible rope. She entered a suite of rooms just off the lobby and I went in after her.

Everything from then on is a little hazy. I didn't

know anything that went on after the succubi showed up and engaged the aliens in the ultimate battle of the sexes because I'd been rendered brainless by the time that came to pass. In fact, I only found out what happened when I talked to the professor later and got his account. As it turned out, he ended up being the sole survivor of the aliens' invasion.

It seems when I started across the street Prof. Jaczlok answered nature's call and went downstairs in the City Hall to use the john. While he was gone, and while I was sneaking in the back way, the aliens sallied forth from the hotel and proceeded to lay everybody who'd remained unscrewed to date and the last of Midvale's citizens joined the ranks of brainless fuckees. But they missed the professor since he wasn't on the scene, and when he came back up it was all over and he was able to witness the final struggle and report on it.

As for my encounter with the female alien, I only remember watching as she moved toward me in a kind of libidinous slow motion, her gown dropping from her shoulders and revealing an unspeakably beautiful body with alabaster skin and perfectly symmetrical curves and long, slim legs and suddenly I was the proud owner of the granddaddy of all hard-ons, a wondrous instrument which pulsed and spat and lunged in anticipation.

We fell together in a mad embrace and I swooned amidst a kind of surreal swirl of pheromones and lust and genitalia and mounds of ripe, melon-like tits and powerful, atavistic yearnings and indescribable excitement, pleasure, and passion.

It was primitive, wild, mad, incredible, astonishing,

warm. The climax was an enormous emptying of everything into everything else, a moment of oneness with all women everywhere, a universal fuck transcending time and place, mind and matter, life and death.

And then it was over. I sat up and looked around and felt a kind of giddiness coupled with a serenity I'd never known before. I dressed and went out and back to the lobby and the aliens were sitting on chairs with a low coffee table pulled up between them They were eating mashed potatoes and gravy and split-pea soup and they took no notice of me as I crossed the lobby and went out onto Main Street.

The professor hurried to my side. "Ah," he said, "you, too! She has taken your brain!"

I grinned at him and wandered off in a happy daze and didn't see him until the next evening when Ellen and I were on our way to Lola's for dinner. My plan had worked. We were ideally suited now, each of us infected with the aliens' strange chemistry and nicely attuned to each other. It was a union made, if not in heaven, at least in the heavens.

The streets were crowded with people, soldiers and feds and cops all over the place. An air of normalcy hung over the town, but it was an air that would never be quite normal again. The professor was coming out of the hotel with a suitcase in his hand and he called to us.

"Mr. Grogan!" he said.

"What's with the suitcase, Professor?" I said.

"I go home now," he said.

"What about the aliens?" Ellen asked.

"They've also gone home," he said. Then, "Ah, but of course, you don't know. It went as I said it would. The succubi appeared and the aliens slept and dreamed. It was a magnificent show! The building rocked like an earthquake and the windows steamed up. The aliens and succubi made love on every floor all night long and at dawn it was quiet, very quiet. Then the aliens came out from the hotel and went away in the Rolls Royce. I called the general and he has opened the town again. Midvale is saved!"

I looked around at the still discernible sappy grins on the faces of my fellow citizens and said, "Are we? Looks more like the aliens won after all."

EPILOGUE

Well, that's how it actually turned out—almost. The Midvale that was there when I arrived, the boring, dying little town infected by terminal ennui did, indeed, die, but it rose again to become a bustling, thriving, upward bound metropolitan center of sybarites with an economy based entirely on pleasures of all kinds with special emphasis on sensual ones.

The government was denounced because it panicked and abandoned an American town to invading space aliens and it felt enough guilt to declare Midvale a federal disaster area and pumped millions into its economy. Farmers were paid handsomely for crops they didn't even plant; Nick at Andy's pool hall was given eleven million dollars and he opened a three-story billiards emporium complete with a hundred shiny, new slot machines; Lola took eighteen million bucks and cut a deal with some New York magnates to build a sixteen-story hotel and casino complex.

And so it went. Almost overnight an array of casinos, brothels, bars and nightclubs, miniature golf courses, restaurants, bowling alleys, and sports stadia sprang up in and around town. The Midvale Manor Hotel was turned into a kind of shrine and people poured into Midvale from all points of the compass to get a gander at the place where real aliens from outer space had attempted to conquer Earth by fucking everybody senseless and had been thwarted by a couple of local spirits.

Chief Hawes got a six million dollar grant and opened a Lexus dealership; Carl Parks built an office complex and took up philandering as a hobby (as did all the rest of us); Docs Gramble and Bane opened their own hospital; Eli stayed on as mayor and made a fortune in graft, and everybody ended up in the chips.

Even the Beacon prospered. Circulation went from a few thousand to a million as people subscribed from all over the world. Bert used a four million dollar grant to expand into printing and publishing and was finally bought out by Rupert Murdoch for untold millions. The whole Beacon staff was cut in for a share, of course, and each grew as rich as Croesus.

And what about yours truly?

I married Ellen and we moved into a twenty-room mansion she built from her profits from buying and selling real estate in Midvale's booming economy, and you won't find a better matched couple anywhere in Christendom. We spend our days in the casinos or idling along the avenues on protracted shopping trips or eating in the best restaurants just like everybody else in Midvale. I smoke twenty-dollar cigars and drink champagne and wear handtailored suits and drive my own white Rolls. All in all, it's a grand life, an easy life, one might even say a dream life.

Of course, one thing was missing to round it out and complete the picture, and even that finally came to pass. I wrote a book—this book—on how we saved the Earth from a race of ruthless fuckers and it was snatched up by a prominent New York publisher for a staggering advance and soared to the top of the bestseller lists in record time. My picture appeared on the cover of Time and Hollywood besieged me with offers for the screen rights and my literary cup runneth over, indeed.

Then one day I was at home lounging poolside with Chief Hawes, Carl, and Eli who'd stopped by for a chat when Ellen stepped out on the patio and said I had a phone call. I picked up the phone and said, "Hello?"

A woman's voice said, "Mr. Grogan? This is Phoebe Swanson. I'm a member of the Pulitzer Prize Committee and I calling to inform you that the Committee has..."

THE END

www.ingramcontent.com/pod-product-compliance
Lightning Source LLC
Chambersburg PA
CBHW051752040426
42446CB00007B/329